"The souls of a million and a half Jewish children murdered in the Holocaust are floating in the air above us. Your task is to give those souls bodies to live in."
—The Ponevezher Rav, Rabbi Yosef Shlomo Kahaneman, as quoted by Rabbi Berel Wein

"The Satmar Rebbe, Rabbi Yoel Teitelbaum, admonished his followers to treat their children well because some of them were the reincarnated souls of their own murdered parents."
—Rabbi Fischel Schachter, international lecturer and author

"In our generation, after the [German] enemies killed approximately one million pure, holy Jewish children, Hashem is now sending these one million children back into our generation. These souls are fiery souls—souls of holy and pure people who were killed for the sanctification of God's name."
—Rav Shalom Noach Berezovsky, *Netivot Shalom*, *Kuntres Haharugah Alayich*

PRAISE FOR
I'VE BEEN HERE BEFORE

"As a son of Holocaust survivors, I learned from an early age that long after the years of my parents' suffering, the nightmares lingered on. In this monumental work, Sara Rigler documents and analyzes the frightening recollections of those who were never actually there, the nightmares of so many born after the Holocaust and raised in the blissful tranquility of the New World. This is an incredibly eye-opening and inspiring journey into one of the greatest mysteries of our times."
—Rabbi Moshe Weinberger,
Rabbi of Congregation Aish Kodesh, Woodmere, NY

"Mrs. Sara Rigler, *tichyeh*, has written an interesting book about persons who were not physically in the Holocaust, but their souls seem to have been there. It might be that they are *gilgulim* of people who died in the Holocaust. It is worthwhile reading."
—Rabbi Avigdor Nebenzahl,
Rosh Yeshivah and Rabbi of the Old City of Jerusalem

"Sara Yoheved Rigler has done exceptional work in meticulously compiling, recording, and describing personal stories of Jews and non-Jews from many countries. By doing so she has rendered an invaluable service not only to the previously 'secret society' of suffering members of the Jewish community by freeing them from a sense of isolation, but also to humanity as a whole by delivering the ultimate proof that reincarnation is a reality—rather than a belief system."
—Sabine Lucas, PhD,
author of *Past Life Dreamwork*

I'VE
BEEN
HERE
BEFORE

ALSO BY SARA YOHEVED RIGLER

Holy Woman

Lights from Jerusalem

Battle Plans: How to Fight the Yetzer Hara
(with Rebbetzin Tziporah Heller)

*God Winked: Tales and Lessons from
My Spiritual Adventures*

Heavenprints

*Emunah with Love and Chicken Soup:
The Story of Rebbetzin Henny Machlis*

I'VE

WHEN SOULS

BEEN

OF THE

HERE

HOLOCAUST RETURN

BEFORE

SARA YOHEVED RIGLER

ISBN: 978-1-61465-575-6
Library of Congress Control Number: 2021939904

Distributed by:
Mekor Press
a division of Menucha Publishers, Inc.
1235 38th Street
Brooklyn, NY 11218
Tel/Fax: 718-232-0856
sales@menuchapublishers.com
www.mekorpress.com

Printed in Israel

Rabbi Zev Leff

Rabbi of Moshav Matityahu
Rosh HaYeshiva—Yeshiva Gedola Matityahu

הרב זאב לף

מרא דאתרא מושב מתתיהו
ראש הישיבה—ישיבה גדולה מתתיהו

D.N. Modiin 71917   Tel: 08-976-1138 'טל   פקס' 08-976-5326 :Fax   ד.נ. מודיעין 71917

Dear Friends,

I have read portions of the manuscript "I've Been Here Before – When Souls of the Holocaust Return" by Sara Yoheved Rigler.

The book is an astounding work that documents accounts of people who have experiences that point to their being reincarnations of souls of individuals who perished in the holocaust. The authoress herself is amongst those who had this experience. Her personal story contained in the book is fascinating.

The book contains a very detailed discussion of reincarnation and presents an accurate rendition of an authentic Jewish perspective on the subject. The many personal accounts of those who have recollection of past lives linked to holocaust victims are not only fascinating and inspiring, but can strengthen one's belief in the soul and afterlife.

The Chofetz Chaim, quoted by Rav Elchonon Wasserman, observed that as the days of Moshiach near all the many heavenly calculations accumulating from the time of creation are going to have to be settled and each soul will have to come to its final tikkun. Based on this, perhaps many of the individuals who perished in the holocaust were themselves reincarnations from previous generations that met their tikkun in this manner.

The book is interesting, inspiring, and literally mind boggling – reminding one of how little we really know about the world and of G-d's plan for it.

I commend Mrs. Rigler, who is an accomplished writer, for providing a quality, well documented, and thorough presentation of this fascinating topic. I pray that Hashem bless her and her family with life, health and the wherewithal to continue to merit the community with her literary talent.

Sincerely,
With Torah blessings

Zev Leff

Rabbi Zev Leff

Kislev 5781

מוסדות אור שמח מרכז טננבאום
רח' שמעון הצדיק 22-28
ירושלים ת.ד. 18103
טל: 0315-581-02

מכתב ברכה

This book is really unique on several counts. First, it deals with an esoteric concept deeply rooted in Kabbalah that is not well understood by the average or even educated Jew, i.e., *gilgul* or the reincarnation of souls. Second, it links this topic to a dark, tragic episode in Jewish history, the Holocaust, and shows how this tragedy continues to inflict its pain on people who were born decades after its conclusion.

The concept of *gilgul* has a controversial history in Judaism. Some eminent thinkers, like Rabbi Saadyah Gaon, rejected it out of hand. Others, like Ramban and all the Kabbalists, deeply believed in this idea and used it as a partial explanation for the suffering of the righteous. While not a definite article of faith, *gilgul neshamot* has become a widely accepted idea within traditional Judaism, and some maintain that it finds some empirical support in the scientific studies of past-life regression.

Sara Rigler, who is both an accomplished writer and a very committed Orthodox Jew (as well as a person of sound mind and judgment!), has written a powerful and gripping narrative detailing the experiences of people who claim to be the reincarnations of Jews who were murdered in the Holocaust. Many of these people have been obsessed with the Holocaust from the time they were children, even though their parents were neither survivors nor even talked about the Nazi atrocities. Even as children, these people had vivid, terrifying dreams or even day visions of torture, persecution, flight, and panic. They often had an unexplained hatred for all things German even when that hatred was not shared by parents, family, friends, or Hebrew school teachers. Aptly described as members of a secret society so secret that even the members didn't know they belong, many of these people felt marginalized, sick, crazy, not normal. They had no idea where these feelings, images, fears, and panics came from until Mrs. Rigler suggested to them that the origin lay in the mystery of *gilgul*. And with that revelation, many felt liberated and were able to go on despite their memories of extreme suffering.

This is heavy stuff, and obviously every reader will have to judge for themselves, but Mrs. Rigler makes a powerful case for her conclusions, and the stories in any case make for fascinating reading. While I can offer no definitive opinion whether her conclusions are true, I can state that her conclusions are consistent with Jewish tradition. Moreover, I myself have heard *gedolim* declare that many of the Jews who have recently returned to Judaism (*chozrei b'teshuvah*) might possibly be the reincarnated souls of those murdered in the Shoah, persons who were either too young to keep mitzvot or who were simply unobservant. God gave them a second chance for *tikkun* (rectification).

Mrs. Rigler has given us much to think about, particularly in seeing the cosmic intergenerational impact of radical evil that transcends all boundaries of time and space. And if evil can have such an effect, it is surely the case that goodness can. Our lives matter and we should make them count!

With admiration and berachah,

Yitzchak A. Breitowitz

Rav, Kehillat Ohr Somayach

This book
is dedicated to the
six million holy Jews
who perished in the Holocaust
and
to the nearly three hundred thousand survivors,
who carried the German Gehinnom with them,
throughout lives that were long or short,
lonely or blessed with descendants,
those many who became great examples for the world,
and those who remained imprisoned in their nightmares.
I have tremendous reverence for them all.

CONTENTS

FOREWORD

by Rebbetzin Tziporah (Heller) Gottlieb

I WAS INITIALLY SKEPTICAL about the relevance of a book on reincarnation. I am very comfortable in the familiar tangible present, and had no desire to cross the border from there into unexplored (and what I thought was unexplorable) territory.

Then I looked again.

The level of solid research I discovered in Sara Yoheved Rigler's book was far beyond anything that I had envisioned. The sheer number of interviews and the consistency that I saw in the narrative of the stories presented by people from every age group, gender, and culture was unexpected, and demanded more than a dismissive shrug. This book is not only credible, it is important.

You come to see that the story of your life doesn't necessarily end when your body dies. The abrupt end to life of the six million isn't the end of their stories either. The riddle of the Holocaust is not solved, nor can it be, but it can now be viewed from another perspective. People who are far greater than I (such as the Amshinover Rebbe, who encouraged Mrs. Rigler to write the book) clearly recognized the need for you to see life as a story with many chapters, and not to judge the entire "book" by one chapter.

I encourage you to read (and no doubt reread) this important and well-written book, to let the stories touch your heart and mind.

ACKNOWLEDGMENTS

M Y DEEPEST GRATITUDE TO:

Hashem Yisbarach, Who gives me the words and the ability to put them together.

The Revered Rebbe of Amshinov, *shlita*, who told me I should write this book. My spiritual connection to the Rebbe sustains me and enables me to thrive.

Rabbi Yitzchak Breitowitz, whose broad knowledge and deep wisdom is matched only by his compassionate heart. I am grateful for his *haskamah* on this book, but even more so for his guidance in my life. He is a glowing example of great intellect combined with generosity of spirit.

Rebbetzin Tziporah (Heller) Gottlieb, my mentor and teacher. For thirty-six years, her brilliance, spiritual depth, humility, humor, and personal example of spiritual striving have enhanced my life. I am grateful for her foreword to this book. She is my example of how a great teacher not only teaches, but also loves her students.

Rabbi Zev Leff, who generously gave of his time to read the book and write a *haskamah*. He responded to my request with an openhearted willingness and alacrity that I can only hope to emulate.

Dr. Sabine Lucas, who generously shared with me her book and film on reincarnation, as well as her own personal experiences. Writing about an unpopular subject can be lonely, but Dr. Lucas's encouragement propelled me forward.

Efim Svirsky, who generously shared accounts of his clients' past lives and who encouraged me in this work. When I started to investigate the dark stories of reincarnated Nazis, he wisely advised me to stop, reminding me that this is a book about the victims, not the perpetrators.

Yael Shahar, whose story and whose life showed me that every past life can be redeemed and used as the raw material for greatness. Her book *Returning* is the queen of this genre.

Carol Bowman, an acclaimed author, who gave generously of her time for interviews and to answer questions.

Rabbi Shlomo Nachman ben Ya'acov, who went beyond his comfort zone in order to share his entire story in a way that would most impact my readers.

Sarah Yehudit Schneider, a distinguished scholar of Kabbalah and Chassidut, who reviewed and approved chapter 2.

Uriela Sagiv, my close friend and literary advisor, who gave suggestions on various chapters. Her help is invaluable in every book I write.

Ruchama King Feuerman, a great writer and friend, who connected me to Fally Klein, an invaluable resource for this book.

Baila (Belinda) Levy, my brilliant and efficient research assistant, who did for me, repeatedly, what I simply could not do for myself.

All of the over 450 people who responded to my online survey or wrote emails to me detailing their experiences. I was not able to use every testimony, but I do value each and every one. Without them this book would have remained nothing more than an imprisoned yearning in my heart.

The following people who gave generously of their time to be interviewed:

Abby Reading
Caron Levy
Chava Dumas
Devora Sinton
Fally Klein
Elise Wardle
Goldie Blumberger
Hanna Sara Zeller
Leeba Braun
Katie Andersson
Miriam Maslin
Mimi Jankowitz
Dr. Miriam Adahan
Morris Srour
Navah Verhoeven
Michel Savanes
Margaret Ann Rice
Junie Maggio
Chavah Fried

Julie Miller
Quintan Wikswo
Stephanie Kraft
Tamarah Chancellor
Josh Kardos
Glenn Hill
Dr. Naomi Greenwald
Morasha Freund
Kate Rose
Sara Argamon
Carol Hallyn
Janet Kasten Friedman
Shaina Buchwald
Dr. Ian Fowler
Kathy Boyer
Claudia Antell
Chiaki Visnyei

Hirsch Traube, the CEO of Menucha Publishers, whose faith in me and in this book gave him the daring to agree to publish a volume on such a controversial subject. May his courage be amply rewarded.

Esther Heller, editor in chief of Menucha Publishers, a kindred soul who knew what to keep and what to delete, and how to turn a literary weed into a flower. It's been a pleasure working with her.

Chaya Baila Lieber, whose meticulous editing and attention to every word, punctuation mark, and footnote awes me. For me, who finds it easier to write an entire chapter than to write one proper footnote, Chaya Baila is a Godsend. She also acted as project manager. I feel blessed to have her on my team.

Sam Schwartz, who designed the cover, a formidable job that he executed with brilliant creativity, artistry, and sensitivity to an almost impossible-to-portray subject.

Deena Weinberg, who did the typesetting and also supplied the amazing sources from the *Netivot Shalom*. Her enthusiasm for this book gave me *chizuk*.

Daliya Shapiro, who did the proofreading with the eye of an eagle and the care of a brain surgeon.

Leib Yaacov Rigler, my husband, who supplied the title, innumerable helpful suggestions, and the *simchas chaim* that makes possible any creative endeavor. He shopped and cooked for Shabbos, thus freeing me to finish writing this book. He also proofread the entire book. This book, like my life, would be a faint shadow of unfulfilled potential without Leib Yaacov.

Yisrael Rohn Rigler, my son the filmmaker, whose documentary based on this book will spread its message throughout the world.

My children and grandchildren, **Yisrael Rohn Rigler, Pliyah Esther and Avraham Cirt**, and **Dovid, Yonaton, Michael, and Shai Lapid Cirt**. This book is about my sometimes-sorrowful past; they are my radiant future.

A Note about the Names
Used in This Book

When a first and last name appears, it is a true name. When only a first name appears, it is a pseudonym.

When I refer to children, I use their names at birth. Many married women have changed their last names, and many converts and *baalei teshuvah* have taken on Hebrew first names by which they are known today.

PART I

THE PAST
PERMEATES
THE PRESENT

PROLOGUE

APRIL, 1969. NEW DELHI. I was a twenty-one-year-old American college student who had just spent my junior year in India. With a Pan Am round-the-world ticket in hand, I made my way to the airline office to book my itinerary home.

After an hour's wait, I took my seat across a desk from a pretty young woman with a long black braid, wearing a blue-and-orange batik sari.

I handed her my ticket and told her, "I want to fly as soon as possible from here to Tel Aviv, then to Stockholm, then Paris, then London, then Philadelphia."

She smiled, and started leafing through a thick tome—the airline's scheduled flights. A couple minutes later, she looked up and announced: "Pan Am does not fly directly from New Delhi to Tel Aviv. But you can get a flight at 2:00 a.m. tonight to Istanbul, and from there fly to Tel Aviv."

"Fine," I said amiably.

"Very good," she said, writing it down. She then started leafing through the tome again. Several minutes later, she looked up and smiled once more. "We have no direct flights from Tel Aviv to Stockholm, but I've found you an excellent connection through Frankfurt. You leave Tel Aviv in the morning, you have two and a half hours to change flights in Frankfurt, and you arrive in Stockholm early in the evening."

"N-n-no, not Frankfurt," I stammered. "Please find me a different connection."

Her smile faded as she looked at me quizzically. "But this is the best connection."

"I don't want to go to Germany," I replied firmly.

"It's just two and a half hours," she explained. "You won't even leave the airport."

I gazed at her. How to tell this young Indian woman, one of a nation 600 million strong, that had resided in its homeland without interruption for at least three thousand years, that as a Holocaust-obsessed child I had vowed never to set foot in Germany? Not even if I had to go hundreds of miles out of my way to go around it. Not Germany. Not ever.

Hatred of Germany was the passion of my growing-up years. Even as a child, I refused to buy any German product, refused to have my picture taken with a German camera, refused to ride in a Volkswagen.

Neither my parents, my brother, nor my friends shared my seething hatred. Born in Camden, New Jersey, in 1948, I had no idea where it came from. No one in our family had been exterminated by the Nazis. I didn't know a single Holocaust survivor until the Schwartzes moved in around the corner from us, and one hot summer day my brother Joey came home and announced that Mrs. Schwartz had a tattooed number on her arm. I had never seen a Holocaust movie. Indeed, there were no Holocaust movies to see in the 1950s and early '60s. What was the root of my passionate hatred of everything German?

At the beginning of ninth grade, I had a dream that began to unravel the mystery for me. Everyone in my ninth-grade class was required to select a language to study for the next three years. Our choices were French, Spanish, German, and Latin. All my friends chose French or Spanish. I chose German. When my surprised friends asked me why, I replied with steely eyes, " 'Know thine enemy.' I want to read *Mein Kampf* in the original."

At the end of my first week of German study, after two classes and a language lab repeating, "*Guten tag, Fraulein Hess,*" I had a convoluted dream. I woke up in the middle of it, shaking. I and everyone else in the dream had been speaking fluent German.

I knew nothing about reincarnation except as jokes about people coming back as animals, but from that dream, I was convinced that I had lived before, in Germany. Perhaps my anger toward and hatred of Germans were fomented by my own nightmarish experience at their hands.

Seven years later, sitting in the Pam Am office in New Delhi, I looked at the pretty clerk and repeated, "Please find me a different connection. Any country except Germany."

Sighing, she turned pages for a few more minutes. Finally, shaking her head, she announced, "The only other connection I can find for you is through Vienna. It's a seven-hour layover, and it gets you into Stockholm at midnight. Is that all right?"

"That will be fine," I said.

That night I flew out of India. After a week in Israel, I landed in Vienna on a sunny, pleasant spring day. My mood matched the weather. Vienna to me conjured up visions of Strauss waltzes and Viennese pastries. And the seven-hour layover was perfect. I would have time to taste the flavor of the city (and its pastries) and then catch my flight to Stockholm, without having to pay for a hotel.

I took the airport bus into the center of the city, a well-manicured commercial area with fine department stores and outdoor cafés. By now I was a seasoned traveler. During my peregrinations throughout India, I had developed my own approach to getting to know a place and its people. I would go to the residential districts, wander around examining the buildings and their use of space (inspired by a book I read about how different cultures use space differently), strike up a conversation with the locals, and often be invited inside to experience the family setting. Eager to start my investigation of Vienna, I caught a local bus heading toward one of the residential neighborhoods.

Some twenty minutes later, I picked a stop at random and alighted. In order not to get lost, I decided to cross the street and walk along the bus route, so I could easily retrace my steps to the bus stop going back to town.

At first, I stood there and examined the architecture: flat-fronted yellowish buildings four stories high with rows of shutterless windows. They were old, but I couldn't tell how old. Certainly before World War II, possibly before World War I.

I walked down the street, pondering what I had learned from my book about the anthropology of space. After a few blocks, I became aware that I was feeling uneasy. The buildings looming above me started to assume a sinister appearance. I came to a corner and crossed the street. As I continued on the other side, I felt a menacing presence issuing from the cross street behind me. I swung around—and saw only an elderly woman walking her dog.

What's wrong with you? I chided myself. *You have almost four hours before you have to be back at the airport. It's a beautiful day. Calm down and enjoy yourself.*

I took a deep breath and resumed walking, trying to concentrate on a litany of cultural indexes: how the other pedestrians were dressed, the frequency of the litter baskets, the nature of the advertisements on the side of a passing bus. But as soon as I crossed the next side street, my heart started to beat wildly and my palms started to sweat. I felt like I couldn't breathe.

This is ridiculous, I told myself. But my feet had already turned around and were carrying me back to the bus stop.

I crossed the side street in the opposite direction. That's when I heard them—a gang of blond-haired, blue-eyed youths laughing raucously, coming down the side street behind me. I quickened my steps. They were calling to me, following me, gaining on me. I broke out into a run. Sweat drenched my blouse, despite the coolness of the day. I could hear them behind me, their laughter now turned to curses and catcalls. A bus passed me and pulled over to the bus stop some twenty meters in front of me. The gang was right behind me, running fast. I sprinted with all my might, and leaped onto the bus just as it started to pull away from the curb.

Only when the bus had closed its door and picked up speed with me safely inside did I turn around to look. The street was empty.

CHAPTER 1

THE SECRET
SOCIETY

THIS SECRET SOCIETY IS SO RECONDITE that most of its members are unaware that they belong. Nevertheless, the membership numbers, perhaps, in the hundreds of thousands. The qualifications for membership are recurring dreams, panic attacks, fearsome flashbacks, or phobias of trains, showers, or uniformed men. Most of its members were born between 1945 and 1961, in North or South America, Europe, or Israel. Although members' individual experiences are unique, the common denominator, the secret handshake of this society, is a childhood obsession with the Holocaust by youths unrelated to Holocaust survivors, who never heard it discussed, who never saw a Holocaust movie until after their dreams, flashbacks, or phobias were already haunting their young lives.

9

One of my youngest respondents, Samantha, was born in Boulder, Colorado, in 1985. She confesses:

> At age eleven, I became obsessed with the Holocaust. I thought of it every waking moment, all while trying to be a "normal child." My obsession was my deepest secret and my deepest shame. I thought something was very wrong with me, and tried in vain to stop thinking about "it." I felt such guilt that I could not forget. I was sure I was the only child who was obsessed with the Holocaust and that no one would like me if they found out.

Most of the members of the Secret Society grew up not believing in reincarnation. The hidden fears, the passions that drove them toward Holocaust books or away from everything German, were inexplicable to themselves. They were like a child suffering from a genetic disease that no one on either side of the family had ever had, only to discover, later in life, that she was adopted. Only this disclosure made sense of the symptoms she suffered.

Born in 1948 in suburban New Jersey to second-generation American Jewish parents with no family connection to the Holocaust, my own disbelief in reincarnation marred my growing-up years in two ways: It left me devoid of any logical explanation for my obsession with the Holocaust and my seething hatred of everything German. And it filled me with anger against God at the suffering of innocent Jews whose final chapter ended in the gas chambers of Auschwitz or the pits of Babi Yar.

I well remember the day in third grade of Hebrew school, at the age of eleven, when I realized that I was not "normal." During recess I was sitting, legs dangling, on the desk of my favorite Hebrew school teacher, Mr. Feinstein. I told him how my father had just purchased a German camera, and of course I refused to let him take my picture with it. I myself refused to buy German products and never accepted a ride in a Volkswagen. Mr. Feinstein asked me if any members of my extended family had been killed in the Holocaust.

"No," I replied.

"Do your parents hate Germans?" he probed.

"I guess not. They never talk about the Holocaust," I answered, clueless as to what he was getting at.

"Then why do you hate Germans so much?"

I stared at him as if he had asked me why I like chocolate milkshakes. "All Jewish kids hate Germans," I replied, stating the obvious.

The bell announced the end of recess. My classmates filed in and took their seats, with me still sitting on the teacher's desk. Mr. Feinstein threw out a question: "How many of you hate Germans?"

My hand shot up. Harry Davidov tentatively half-lifted his hand. No one else in the class moved.

Mr. Feinstein gazed at me without saying a word. I slithered down from his desk, feeling weird, estranged from my friends, a different species, an ugly duckling.

How could it be that my inner furies were not what all Jewish kids felt? Where *did* they come from? Who had given birth to them? The genealogy of my innermost passions was suddenly shrouded in haze.

Trying to understand myself without a concept of reincarnation was like trying to put together a jigsaw puzzle with half the pieces missing.

As my mentor, Rebbetzin Tziporah (Heller) Gottlieb, is wont to say: Assessing any individual life is like reading page 326 to page 392 in a 500-page book. You don't know what came before or what will come afterwards. How can you possibly understand what's going on?

For some members of the Secret Society, their Holocaust-related dreams, phobias, and flashbacks are an occasional dark intruder into their otherwise sunlit life. For others, the Holocaust is a malevolent phantom that haunts their every night for years or decades. One woman born in Israel in 1979 had nightmares every night from her early childhood until she went for a past-life regression at the age of twenty-nine.

"Growing up, during my primary years, I always had nightmares," she wrote to me. "I would wake up very scared along with heart palpitations.... In my teenage years I remember more. There wasn't a night where I would not wake up from a nightmare to do with the Holocaust." After her catharsis during her past-life regression (see chapter 7), she never had another nightmare.

For still other members of the Secret Society, the malevolent phantom lurks in the corner of their days, an ominous presence always in the periphery of their conscious mind. Diana Lubarsky was born in Brooklyn in 1945 to a Jewish family with no connection to the Holocaust. In her late twenties, after the birth of her first child, she started having

Holocaust-related nightmares and déjà-vu experiences, such as tollbooths turning into checkpoints, "constantly, constantly, constantly." With no formal artistic training, Diana began sculpting the detailed images she saw, and has produced an impressive collection of sculptures, exhibited at the Florida Holocaust Museum and other places.

"The sudden and urgent need to sculpt arrived only after the Holocaust Images began," Diana wrote on her website, Holocaustimages.com. "As image after image seared across my mind, the need to create that which I 'saw' became overwhelming.... For more than a quarter of a century these images have been with me and have bound me so deeply to the Holocaust that it has infused itself into every aspect of my life."

Diana's description of her dual life is chilling:

> For more than thirty years the images of the Holocaust have lived behind my eyes. It is like having one world superimposed upon another. In my normal, everyday world I am a wife, a mother, a professional physical therapist. I am involved with my family, friends, coworkers, and patients. I volunteer, cook and bake, and host gatherings and parties that fill my house with people and laughter.
>
> And then there is my other world. At any time, day or night (though usually during the late evening hours), an entirely different world comes into focus behind my eyes, as a never-ending ragtag line of people trudges slowly and endlessly across the fabric of my life. I see them as clearly as I see my own hands.

For souls like Diana Lubarsky, to refer to the Holocaust as their "past life" is a misnomer.

One afternoon, a few years after I moved to Jerusalem, I was sitting on my living room couch speaking with my friend Hanna Sara Zeller. For the first time in my life, I felt safe to share my secret. I told her that I was convinced that I am a soul who perished in the Holocaust. She looked at me wide-eyed. "So am I!" she confided, and went on to tell me about a vision she had had nightly when she was four years old.

Every night after her mother tucked her in and left her to go to sleep, little Jackie, as she was known then, would stare into her pillow as if it were a TV set, and see a scene. She saw herself inside the back of a truck filled with women. Some of them were collapsing to the floor. Then she saw herself fly out of the truck. There, above the truck, she would feel a sense of liberation, and say, "I got out. I'm free now."

Since Jackie had been born in 1950 to American parents who never discussed the Holocaust, as a child she had no way to understand this strange, unsettling vision. Only decades later did she learn that the Nazis' earliest experiment in mass murder was to pack people into a truck and pipe the carbon monoxide gas from the motor into the back of the truck.

Many years later, Hanna Sara told me, she was teaching a fourth-grade class in a Jewish day school in Connecticut. In the library, leafing through a Holocaust book for young readers, she found a watercolor sketch of women standing inside the back of a truck. "Standing in the library," she recounted, "I felt like a lightning bolt of recognition hit me."

Sitting on my living room couch listening to Hanna Sara, I realized that my secret was not peculiar to me. Since that day in Hebrew school at the age of eleven, I had felt odd and isolated. Of course, I would not let down the guise of my intellectual/ sensible persona to expose the improvable presumption that I dared to include myself with the Eli Weisels and Viktor Frankls, with the legions of survivors whose tattooed numbers testified to suffering a thousand times more real and terrible than mine. Their suffering was Everest compared to my ant-hill. No, I was not in their fellowship.

Yet, sitting next to Hanna Sara, I realized that I was part of a different fellowship. She and I—and how many others—were souls of the Holocaust returned. We were the "not-survivors." Our childhoods in the security and comfort of post-War America were a split-level suburban house built on a basement full of horrors. Growing up in that sprawling neighborhood of split-level houses with manicured lawns, I had not known how many others had a basement like mine.

From that day on, I shared my secret with other good friends, American-born Jewish women living in Jerusalem. Every one of them responded by revealing their own secret conviction of their Holocaust past. Anna, from the age of five, had had a recurring dream that she was being tortured in a laboratory setting by a man in a military uniform and a white-coated doctor, whom many years later she identified as Dr. Mengele. Eva had had a childhood penchant for hiding in small spaces and not coming out when the game of hide-and-seek was over, feeling that her life depended on staying hidden.

It took another two decades, after I had already established credibility as a serious writer, for me to come out of the closet and publish two articles about Holocaust reincarnations. I also composed a questionnaire for those who had reasons to believe that they were reincarnated from the Holocaust, and posted the questionnaire on my website and my Facebook page.

Among my 2,700 "Facebook friends," the vast majority of whom are strangers to me, several dozen filled out my questionnaire. One of them answered the first question, "When and where were you born?" with "1948, New York." She went on to fill in other answers, about her lifelong obsession with the Holocaust, about her dreams and aversions.

The final question asks for name and email address. I read her reply with consternation. This was my second cousin Eleanor! I had known Eleanor all my life. We had played together as children. We have been in email correspondence for years. We had even met for lunch a few years ago, when I had a speaking engagement in Miami, and had a deep, personal conversation. Yet I had never had an inkling that she, too, was a member of this Secret Society of Holocaust souls.

At the end of my two articles on "Reincarnation and the Holocaust," I appealed: "Readers who have stories alluding to a Holocaust incarnation are invited to send them to the author." Among the hundreds of emails to my website, I read the frequent refrain: "After reading your article on reincarnation and the Holocaust, I felt 'normal' for the first time in my life."

Jacklynn Pincus was born in New York in 1960 to an American father and a French Jewish mother whose parents had been killed in Auschwitz. She wrote to me:

> I was so happy to read your article about reincarnation and the Holocaust because I thought I was alone with these memories. Almost since I was old enough to talk, I have been telling my family that I was an Italian Jew killed in the Holocaust. I have always known this, and it has always been fact to me because I voiced it when I was young. I first gave voice to this memory when I was only five or six years old. At that time, I knew nothing about the Holocaust. When I told my mother this, she was extremely upset and thought I was crazy.

Another American Jewish woman, her father an Ethiopian Jew and her mother descended from Confederate German Jews, is a scholar of "Jews of color." She wrote to me about her traumatic past-life memories that occurred to her spontaneously at the age of two. (For more on the spontaneous past-life memories of young children, see chapter 7.) She also described a panic attack she had at the age of fourteen when visiting in Nebraska and she heard a "European-type siren."

She concluded her account:

> I don't usually discuss these memories or strong feelings; I have for many years worked with survivors in reparation matters and such, and I'm sure they would not accept this at all. I also have twice

married into survivor families, one German, the other Hungarian, and they would think me quite mad if I ever mentioned any of it.... In any event, I will now perhaps stifle those thoughts less, to be able to share them with you or just myself.

A Christian woman from Wisconsin wrote to me describing her detailed Holocaust-related dreams. She continued:

In my second year at university, at age twenty-eight (I was a very late bloomer, I guess), I took a class on the Holocaust (this was a subject barely touched upon in public school). And finally, my dreams made sense. I never shared my information with my professor. I feared appearing rude or crazy. The only explanation that seemed logical to me was that I'd been there in a former life. But I am very hesitant to share this with people in general; I don't want to seem like I am trying to appropriate a history that doesn't truly belong to me. I do not want to make less of the living people (or the dead, for that matter) who have already endured so many indignities. So it has more or less been a secret.

I never thought there were others like myself out there; I never met anyone else who has had the experiences I had. To my astonishment and relief, here you are!

Another woman, born in America in 1946, sent me a detailed account of a recurring nightmare she had from the age of four. "I've stopped talking about reincarnation. Then, today, I read your article. I tried a couple of times throughout my life to tell people that I thought I had lived before, that I died during the Holocaust." Always her disclosures were met with opprobrium.

My brother, a physician in New Jersey, does not believe in reincarnation because he maintains that it is self-aggrandizing. "Everyone thinks he was Julius Caesar," my brother says. "No one thinks he was a galley slave." Every account in this book disproves his assertion. The past lives and deaths—emaciated and humiliated—reported here batter rather than bolster the ego. For these souls, shards of the humiliation inflicted by the Nazis have resurfaced as the shame inflicted by a society that discounts their nightmares as subconscious symbolic ramblings and dismisses their inner torment as the hallucinations of an overactive imagination.

The closet is crowded with people who fear exposing their haunting experiences to mockery and disdain. As one well-known media personality who answered my survey with descriptions of her Holocaust-related dreams explained when she declined to let me use her name: "I am retired now and I don't want any trouble." One purpose of this book is to open the closet door and allow these thousands—or hundreds of thousands—of people to emerge into the daylight of respectability and acceptance.

CHAPTER 2

IS REINCARNATION REAL?

AFTER WORLD WAR II, the esteemed Ponevezher Rav, Rabbi Yosef Shlomo Kahaneman, used to visit Miami annually in order to raise funds for his yeshivah. Rabbi Berel Wein, who was a congregational rabbi in Miami during that period, relates this story:

> One day the Ponevezher Rav called me and asked me to arrange a meeting in my home with all of the younger couples affiliated with my congregation. I told him that I would do so, but I cautioned him that I did not think that he would raise much money from them. He gently told me that he was not going to speak to them about donations at all.
>
> At that meeting, which was very well attended, the Ponevezher Rav rose and said to them: "My

beloved children, the souls of a million and a half Jewish children murdered in the Holocaust are floating in the air above us. Your task is to give those souls bodies to live in."[1]

What is the Jewish approach to reincarnation? Called *gilgul neshamot* (revolving of souls) in Judaism, reincarnation is never explicitly mentioned in the Torah, yet it is a basic principle of Kabbalistic tradition, which stretches back to the Talmudic era. Throughout Jewish tradition, Kabbalah is referred to as *sod*, or secret; the very definition of "secret" is that it is not openly revealed. Thus, for many centuries, written references to reincarnation were cryptic and oblique.

Onkelus, in the first century CE, makes an offhand reference to reincarnation. He translates into Aramaic the Torah verse, "Let Reuven live and not die..." (*Devarim* 33:6) to mean that Reuven should merit the World to Come directly, without having to die again due to reincarnation.

The Ramban, the great thirteenth-century commentator and Kabbalist, taught that certain Biblical verses are based on recognizing reincarnation. For example, the mitzvah of *yibum* (levirate marriage)—that the brother (or closest relative) of a man who died childless must marry the man's widow—is based on the idea that such a marriage allows the soul of the deceased brother to reincarnate in the child born from this marriage. The first mention of *yibum* in the Torah is found in the story of Yehudah, who, upon the death of his eldest son,

---

1. Rabbi Berel Wein, *Personal Memories of Great Men: Rabbi Yosef Shlomo HaKohen Kahaneman*. CD-ROM. The Destiny Foundation.

Er, directed his second son, Onan, to marry Tamar, Er's widow. The Ramban, in his lengthy commentary on this verse, writes that when Yehudah "received this mystical concept from his ancestors, he was quick to fulfill it." At the conclusion of his comment, the Ramban hints, "He who possesses esoteric knowledge will understand this."

In his commentary on the book of *Iyov*, the Ramban is more explicit. On the verse, "God does all these things twice or three times with a man, to bring back his soul from the pit…" (*Iyov* 33:29–30), the Ramban writes that this refers to *gilgul neshamot*.[2]

The *Zohar*, the primary text of Kabbalah, ascribed to the first-century sage Rabbi Shimon Bar Yochai, is replete with references to reincarnation.

The Abarbanel, who lived in Spain in the fifteenth century, was a vocal proponent of reincarnation. He was not a Kabbalist, and he argued that *gilgul neshamot* should not be considered a secret doctrine, reserved for adepts in Kabbalah.[3]

With the emergence of the greatest Kabbalist, the Arizal (Rabbi Yitzchak Luria) in the sixteenth century, the concept of *gilgul neshamot* went from being whispered to being sung out loud. The Arizal's book, *Shaar HaGilgulim*,[4] with intricate complexity identifies "soul sparks" of certain Biblical characters that reincarnated into others. For example, both the souls

---

2. For many other allusions to reincarnation in the Biblical text, see *Return Again*, by Rabbi Avraham Arieh Trugman (Ohr Chadash, 2008).

3. See Abarbanel, *Commentary on the Torah*, Devarim 25.

4. The Arizal's teachings were compiled and published after his death by his disciple Rabbi Chaim Vital.

of Tamar and Tziporah reincarnated into the Judge Devorah. Soul sparks of Avraham's brother Haran reincarnated in Aharon, the first *kohen gadol* (high priest). According to the Arizal, Aharon was not punished for his part in the sin of the golden calf until he was reincarnated as Eli the High Priest, several generations later.

While the Arizal's teachings opened the subject of *gilgul neshamot* to forthright scholarly discourse, two centuries later the Baal Shem Tov made the concept part of popular Jewish culture. Reincarnation became a staple of Chassidic stories and the hashkafic underpinning for understanding why good people suffer.

An example: A couple finally gave birth to a son after years of marriage, but shortly after his brit (circumcision ceremony), the baby died. The bereft parents went to the Baal Shem Tov and asked him why this tragedy had occurred to them. The Baal Shem Tov answered that their child bore the soul of Avraham ben Avraham, a Polish prince who had defied his family and the law of his country by converting from Catholicism to Judaism. He became a devout and saintly Jew, but eventually Polish officials discovered him and put him to death.

The Baal Shem Tov explained that the convert Avraham's only regret was that he had not undergone circumcision on the eighth day, as the Torah commands. His holy soul was therefore permitted to come back as this couple's baby. As soon as his soul was placated by the mitzvah of brit milah, it was free to return to the World of Souls. Because this couple was so virtuous, they had merited to receive such a holy soul, albeit briefly.

Although the Baal Shem Tov and the Vilna Gaon, the eighteenth-century progenitor of today's Lithuanian Chareidi world, differed on many issues, they both accepted *gilgul neshamot* as a given. The same century saw the Ramchal (Rabbi Moshe Chaim Luzzato) explain in his universally admired classic *The Way of God*:

> God arranged matters so that man's chances of achieving ultimate salvation should be maximized. A single soul can be reincarnated a number of times in different bodies, and in this manner, it can rectify the damage done in previous incarnations. Similarly, it can also achieve perfection that was not attained in its previous incarnations.[5]

It is important to note that the Jewish concept of *gilgul neshamot* differs from the concept of reincarnation in Eastern religions. The latter conceive of a single soul entity leaving one body and later coming down intact into another body. The Jewish concept is that a body contains many soul levels and soul sparks. Only unrectified soul sparks return in a new body, for the purpose of *tikkun* (rectification).[6] The rectified soul sparks, having achieved their mission, remain in the higher worlds. A person can simultaneously contain soul sparks from more than one person who lived before. Kabbalah also has copious teachings about *ibbur*, components of a rectified departed soul that attach themselves to

---

5. *The Way of God*, Part 2, 3:10. Translation by Aryeh Kaplan (New York: Feldheim Publishers, 1983), p. 125.

6. See Part II of this book for an exploration of *tikkun* in souls of the Holocaust.

a living person in order to help that person achieve his/her mission.

The most erudite opponent of the concept of reincarnation was Rav Saadyah Gaon, the tenth-century Babylonian sage and philosopher. He famously rejected the concept of reincarnation, objecting that it came from foreign cultures. In his book *Emunos V'Dei'os*, the word Rabbi Saadyah Gaon uses for reincarnation is not *gilgul neshamot*, but rather *ha'atakah*, which comes from the root word meaning "to move" or "to uproot."[7] Contemporary Kabbalist Rabbi Yitzchak Ginsburgh has pointed out that this difference in terminology is significant because *ha'atakah* is best translated as "transmigration" rather than "reincarnation." Transmigration is the Eastern concept mentioned above, where a whole soul returns intact to a new body. *Gilgul neshamot*, on the other hand, is a different spiritual process.

Rabbi Avraham Arieh Trugman, a student of Rabbi Ginsburgh, gives a glimpse of the complexity of the Jewish concept: "*Gilgul* is predicated on understanding that every soul contains many different levels, some active and others relatively dormant. In addition, every soul is connected to higher and more inclusive soul roots."[8]

In any case, *gilgul neshamot* has become part of mainstream Torah Judaism to such an extent that the esteemed Ponevezher Rav, Rabbi Yosef Shlomo Kahaneman, who was neither a Kabbalist nor a Chassid, could beseech young couples in the

---

7. This section is based on Rabbi Avraham Arieh Trugman's *Return Again* (Ohr Chadash, 2008).

8. *Return Again*, p. 32.

1950s to provide bodies for "the souls of a million and a half Jewish children murdered in the Holocaust floating in the air above us." The Klausenberger Rebbe, Rabbi Yekusiel Yehudah Halberstam, himself a survivor who lost his wife and all eleven of his children in the Holocaust, in 1970 told someone interviewed for this book that so many Jewish souls from the Holocaust want to return, and there are not enough Jewish mothers to receive them, so they are going to non-Jewish mothers.[9]

During the last few decades, other Chassidic rebbes have been quoted as saying that the tens of thousands of *baalei teshuvah* (Jews who were raised in secular families and then chose to live a Torah-observant life) are reincarnated souls from the Holocaust. For example, in his modern classic *Netivot Shalom*, the Slonimer Rebbe, Rabbi Shalom Noach Berezovsky, cites the Talmudic story of four hundred boys and girls captured during the Roman conquest of Judea in the first century. They were put on a ship bound for Rome, to be exploited for degenerate purposes.

> The children realized what they were being taken for, and wondered, "If we [throw ourselves] into the sea, will we merit life in the World to Come?"
>
> The oldest among them told them: "Hashem said, 'I will bring back from Bashan, I will bring back from the depths of the sea' [*Tehillim* 68:23]," and all four hundred children jumped into the sea and drowned. The holy books tell us that these four hundred children were sent once again to this world in order to complete their lives, and in the merit of

9. See chapter 8, "Jewish Souls in Christian Bodies."

their great self-sacrifice, they received Divine spiritual levels that made them into great people.

In our generation as well, after the [German] enemies killed approximately one million pure, holy Jewish children, Hashem is now sending these one million children back into our generation. These souls are fiery souls—souls of holy and pure people who were killed for the sanctification of God's name.

This will also enable us to understand the wondrous phenomenon of the *baalei teshuvah* in our generation—a phenomenon that also has no natural explanation. How is it that so many people, some of whom were at the top of the secular pyramid, are leaving all the status and honor they had had behind, and coming to join Hashem's service while demonstrating incredible greatness and self-sacrifice?! As we explained, these are fiery souls that had already been killed for the sanctification of God's name, and were now sent back to this world. These souls truly are on greater spiritual levels, and so their eyes are opened, and they see things and hear things differently.[10]

The *Netivot Shalom* also makes it clear that reincarnation is an ontological necessity, given that the soul is the main constituent of a Jew, and, as a *chelek Eloka mima'al* (a Divine part from Above), it is eternal. "The body lives with the present alone," he writes, "and with no connection to the past that was before it was formed or all that will be after it will conclude its

---

10. *Netivot Shalom, Kuntres Haharugah Alayich*, p. 29, translated by Deena Weinberg.

existence in this world. But the soul of a Jew is eternal. It has a past, and for the most part it is not its first time being in this world; it has a present, and it has a future."[11]

Unlike Jewish acceptance of reincarnation, Western thought, both Christian and secular, have waged a war against the very idea.

The Christian Church and its many denominations consider reincarnation a doctrine of the Devil, in direct contradiction to the dogma of eternal heaven and hell. Origen of Alexandria, a third-century systematic theologian, taught the concept of reincarnation. The Church declared his teachings heresy in 553 and has never reversed that condemnation. In 1600, the Inquisition burned Giordano Bruno at the stake for his heresy in teaching reincarnation.

Even into the nineteenth century, the West's rejection of reincarnation was so absolute that the philosopher Arthur Schopenhauer pejoratively defined Europe as the one part of the world that did not subscribe to belief in reincarnation: "Were an Asiatic to ask me for a definition of Europe, I should be forced to answer him: It is that part of the world completely dominated by the outrageous and incredible delusion that a man's birth is his beginning and that he is created out of nothing."[12]

---

11. Ibid., p. 44, translated by Deena Weinberg.

12. Arthur Schopenhauer, "Parerga und Paralipomena," in *Sämtliche Werke in fünf Bänden im Schuber*, vol. 2 (Leipzig: F. U. Brockhaus), p. 395.

Schopenhauer no doubt agreed with the eighteenth-century writer Voltaire: "It is no more surprising to be born twice than to be born once."

The twentieth century started to see cracks in the wall. Although all major Christian denominations officially reject the concept of reincarnation as being contrary to their belief in one death leading to an eternal heaven or hell, many individual Christians, both clerics and laypeople, espouse belief in reincarnation. A Pew survey of 2018 found that 33 percent of American adults, including 29 percent of Christians, believe in reincarnation. A 2018 study in the UK by the public theology think tank Theos reported that 27 percent of British people believe in reincarnation. Even among churchgoing European Catholics, according to the European Values Study of 1981, 31 percent expressed a belief in reincarnation.

Still, so strong is the reincarnation taboo in the West that Carl Gustav Jung, arguably the most impactful psychologist of the mid-twentieth century, was afraid to admit his belief in it. Jung was the analyst of Erlo Van Waveren, his student and patron, from 1950 until Jung's death in 1961. According to Van Waveren, the analysis revolved mostly around his past-life dreams and visions. In one session, Jung disclosed to Van Waveren his own former lives. "The next morning," Van Waveren recounted in a filmed interview in 1985, "Mrs. Jung came to me at the [Jung] Institute and said, 'Professor Jung said that you can't say a word about what he told you.'"

Van Waveren kept Jung's secret for two decades. According to Jungian analyst Dr. Sabine Lucas, Jung's family and publisher made sure he deleted all references to reincarnation from his autobiographical work, *Memories, Dreams, Reflections*, lest his sterling reputation be tarnished. When questioned directly about whether any of his patients had had dreams suggesting a past life, Jung answered in the negative.

In Van Waveren's 1979 memoir, *Pilgrimage to the Rebirth*, however, he spoke frankly about Jung's decade-long work with him to analyze his past-life dreams. The book was ignored by the Jung Institute, so in 1984–85, shortly before his death, Van Waveren made a last-ditch effort to make reincarnation respectable in the intellectual circles that adulated Jung. Believing strongly that a successful analysis must include traumas from a person's previous lives, Van Waveren did three filmed interviews detailing Jung's belief in reincarnation.

The films lay on a shelf for almost thirty years until Dr. Sabine Lucas, who has worked extensively with past-life dreams throughout her career as a Jungian analyst, discovered them. In 2018, she released on YouTube a feature-length film entitled *A Row of Tombs*. Dr. Lucas uses excerpts from the Van Waveren interviews, veiled quotes from Jung himself, and other evidence to prove that Jung subscribed to reincarnation.

Dr. Brian Weiss, a Yale graduate, was chairman of the Department of Psychiatry at Mount Sinai Medical Center in Miami when he treated a patient he could not help through any of the conventional methods of psychiatry. Finally, he decided to hypnotize her to discover what was probably a repressed trauma from her early childhood. In their second hypnosis session, Dr. Weiss asked the patient to go back to the time when her symptoms started. She found herself in the ancient Near East and spoke in detail about the herbs she was using to prepare bodies for embalming. In subsequent sessions, she reported other past lives. Although her symptoms began to dramatically improve, Dr. Weiss was skeptical about her purported past lives until, during another hypnosis session, she channeled messages about Dr. Weiss's deceased father and infant son that she had absolutely no way of knowing.

After a few months of past-life regressions, the patient was totally cured of her phobias, depression, recurrent nightmares, and panic attacks.

Dr. Weiss writes: "I was hesitant to let other people know about these profound experiences because I was afraid I would be considered 'crazy' or 'weird' by colleagues and friends. On the other hand, I had received further confirmation of the effectiveness of past-life therapy by successfully treating more patients with this technique."[13]

Like any good scientist, Dr. Weiss retreated to the medical library to find validation from other psychiatrists who, like himself, had surely stumbled on past-life recall during sessions of patient hypnosis. Other than the research of Dr. Ian Stevenson, he found nothing.

> At that time I could only wonder whether other psychotherapists were as hesitant as I was to come forward. My research of the literature complete, I was torn between the power and reality of my own direct experiences and the fear that my ideas and

---

13. Brian L. Weiss, MD, *Through Time into Healing* (New York: Touchstone, 1992), p. 36.

new beliefs about life after death...might not be personally and professionally "appropriate."[14]

It took Dr. Weiss seven years to have the courage to go public with his experiences of patients' past lives. His book *Many Lives, Many Masters* became an international best seller. After its publication, he received letters from "psychiatrists and psychologists throughout the country who had experiences like mine but had not dared to make them public."[15]

In my questionnaire for those who had claimed experiences suggestive of a Holocaust incarnation, one question asked, "Growing up, did you believe in reincarnation?" Well over half answered, "No" or "Not sure."

The fear of being tainted by belief in reincarnation was an asset in my research for this book. Initially, I was worried that, drawn by the sensationalism of the concept, people would fabricate dreams and phobias. When I appealed to my readers to send me their experiences alluding to a Holocaust incarnation, how could I ensure that their submissions were authentic?

Instead of a rush of responses by notoriety seekers, I received responses from people as reluctant as if I had asked for kleptomaniacs to come forward. Half refused to let me use their real names. Jerry Friedman, a seventy-two-year-old rabbi who teaches in an American yeshivah, wrote: "I have never shared the following story with anyone, not even my

---

14. Ibid., p. 37.
15. Ibid., p. 39.

parents, wife, or closest friends." After describing in detail a recurrent childhood nightmare, he concluded, "I wish to remain anonymous. Jerry Friedman was the first fictitious name that popped into my head." So concerned was he that he not be viewed as odd for considering his recurrent Holocaust nightmare an actual memory that even the Gmail address from which he wrote to me was created only for this one correspondence.

Another indication of the veracity of the accounts is that each one is unique. I had expected to hear dream after dream of gas chambers and movie-like descriptions of being forced into cattle cars. Instead, less than 40 out of 446 accounts describe dying in the gas chambers. The others describe running in forests or hiding or being suffocated by other bodies after being shot and falling into a pit. Most are unique accounts, such as the one who reported being shot by Italian Blackshirts who invaded his villa.

This book does not claim to be a scientific study. I have relied on personal accounts—dreams, flashbacks, panic attacks, and so on—that cannot be independently verified. The most convincing evidence of the veracity of the accounts is what I call "No Other Rational Explanation," or NORE. This means that when a very young child gives vivid descriptions of a Holocaust scene before he or she could possibility have been exposed to books or movies about the Holocaust, there is no other rational explanation to account for their experiences. Particularly convincing is the testimony of people born into non-Jewish families in places where Jews did not live. Their vivid childhood descriptions of Holocaust scenes could not be traced to either genetic memory or family discussions.

The only scientific studies of reincarnation were conducted by the late Professor Ian Stevenson, MD, who was chairman of the Department of Psychiatry at the University of Virginia School of Medicine, and his successor at the university, Professor Jim B. Tucker. Professor Stevenson authored some three hundred scientific papers and fourteen books on reincarnation. In an interview with the BBC,[16] he explained that early in his medical career he became dissatisfied with modern theories of personality because they could not account for many of the symptoms he encountered in his patients.

He started doing research mainly in India, Sri Lanka, and Burma, where reincarnation is universally accepted, with very young children (two to five years of age) who spoke about who they had been "before." Either Professor Stevenson or researchers working on his behalf interviewed the children and their parents and noted as many details as possible from the children's accounts, such as names of specific places and people. They then went to the village or town indicated and searched for someone who had died who fit the descriptions.

For example, a toddler in Sri Lanka heard her mother mention the distant town of Kataragama and proceeded to tell her mother that she had drowned there when her "dumb" brother pushed her into the river. She went on to mention thirty details of her previous home, family, and neighborhood. Professor Stevenson went to Kataragama and found a family that perfectly fit the child's description. Their two-year-old

---

16. "The Reincarnation Man," interview with BBC on YouTube, posted in December 2013, but recorded "decades earlier."

daughter had indeed drowned in the river while playing with her mentally challenged brother. Professor Stevenson verified twenty-seven of the thirty statements made by the child. Using this method, he meticulously studied the memories of previous lives of some three thousand children, and claimed 90 percent accuracy in their accounts.

The scientific community largely ignored Stevenson's work. However, one eminent scientist, physicist Doris Kuhlmann-Wilsdorf, winner of many awards, including the prestigious Heyn Medal from the German Society for Material Sciences, declared that Stevenson's work had established that "the statistical probability that reincarnation does in fact occur is so overwhelming...that cumulatively the evidence is not inferior to that for most if not all branches of science."[17]

Toward the end of his life, Professor Stevenson turned his attention to cases of reincarnation in Europe, including two children who spoke about Holocaust-like experiences. David Llewelyn was born in 1970 in Chester, England. His mother, Susan, was a Welsh Christian and his biological father was Jewish, but had met David only a few times. As a young child, David had nightmares of large, dark holes filled with corpses, accompanied by people with guns and the stench of dead bodies. These nightmares left David shaking in fear. He also complained of an unusual odor in his bedroom. While Susan cooked with an electric stove, one day they visited an aunt who cooked with gas. David said the gas

---

17. Jesse Bering, "Ian Stevenson's Case for the Afterlife: Are We 'Skeptics' Really Just Cynics?" *Scientific American*, November 2, 2013, https://blogs.scientificamerican.com/bering-in-mind/ian-stevensone28099s-case-for-the-afterlife-are-we-e28098s-kepticse28099-really-just-cynics/.

smelled "like the smell in my room at night. It's going to smother me." David also had waking images of "camps" filled with bald, skeleton-like people, wearing "stripey things."

Most perplexing, when David learned to read and write, he would read and write from right to left, as if he was writing Hebrew or Yiddish. Despite the best efforts of his teachers, David continued sporadically to write from right to left until he was eleven years old. When he drew pictures, he always included a star, even while later exhibiting a phobia of stars. According to his mother, David had a "hatred" of the color yellow, suggestive of the yellow stars the Nazis required Jews to wear. Strangest of all, as a young child David questioned his mother about whether the food she was serving had blood in it. Kosher meat must be salted and soaked to remove the blood, but David had never been exposed to kosher laws in this lifetime.

After interviewing both Susan and David, Professor Stevenson wrote:

> Susan expressed confidence that David showed his unusual behavior related to Jewish customs and his knowledge of concentration camps before he could have had any exposure to relevant information on television. She was sure that nothing discussed in the family could have stimulated his behavior or furnished information for it.[18]

After noting that many of David's memories and the fears that accompanied them persisted into adulthood, Professor

---

18. Ian Stevenson, *European Cases of the Reincarnation Type* (North Carolina: McFarland, 2003), p. 98.

Stevenson concludes his study of David Llewelyn:

> Even supposing that David, at an extremely early age, had learned normally about concentration camps in which millions of Jews and other persons were killed in the early 1940s, we should still need to account for the intense and prolonged effect such knowledge had on him. I believe this case inexplicable by environmental influences and inheritance. Even the most ardent geneticist would not suggest that genes would transmit the habit of reading and writing from right to left, concern about whether the food had blood in it, and images of a concentration camp.[19]

This is what I call NORE (No Other Rational Explanation), which is the basis for the credibility of this book.

Of course, admitting to reincarnation is tantamount to admitting that there is an immortal soul that outlives the physical body, and thus the reluctance of many people to even examine the research of Professor Stevenson. The wrestling match between skepticism and intellectual honesty can be witnessed in a *Scientific American* online article of November 2013, aptly entitled, "Ian Stevenson's Case for the Afterlife: Are We 'Skeptics' Really Just Cynics?"

I was as surprised to read an article about reincarnation in *Scientific American* as I would have been to find a recipe for chicken in a vegan cookbook. In fact, the article's author, Jesse Bering, a former professor of psychology and a self-proclaimed skeptic, seemed even more surprised to be

---

19. Ibid., p. 99.

writing it. "If you're anything like me," he writes, "with eyes that roll over to the back of your head whenever you hear words like 'reincarnation' or 'parapsychology'...."

Nevertheless, after reading Ian Stevenson's research reports, Jesse Bering grudgingly admits:

> I must say, when you actually read them firsthand, many are exceedingly difficult to explain away by rational, non-paranormal means.
>
> I'd be happy to say it's all complete and utter nonsense—a moldering cesspool of irredeemable, anti-scientific drivel. The trouble is, it's not entirely apparent to me that it is. So why aren't scientists taking Stevenson's data more seriously? The data don't "fit" our working model of materialistic brain science, surely. But does our refusal to even *look* at his findings, let alone to debate them, come down to our fear of being wrong? "The wish *not* to believe," Stevenson once said, "can influence as strongly as the wish to believe."

Twice I asked the editor of Aish.com, the popular Jewish website where I am a featured writer, to let me write an article about reincarnation and the Holocaust. Each time he absolutely refused. He would no more have an article about reincarnation than about fairies or flying saucers. Then, in November 2013, armed with this *Scientific American* article, I again asked for permission to write about reincarnation and the Holocaust. Loathe to be more scientifically scrupulous than the *Scientific American*, he reluctantly agreed. My article garnered 3,300 Facebook shares and 160 comments, about a third of which related the writers' own experiences suggesting a Holocaust incarnation.

Often a person who has experiences that point to a past life will clutch at other explanations. A commenter to my Aish.com article, Tiffany Raymond-Snyder, a Christian, wrote:

> I am the farthest removed person from the [Holocaust]. I constantly have dreams and awake visions where I experience concentration camp life and feel extreme heartache when the Holocaust is mentioned. Whenever someone is watching a show on television or has mentioned these facts, I feel nauseous. In high school on a field trip to the [Holocaust] museum in Washington, DC, I was taken outside because of a breakdown. I am not Jewish and only know what I have researched myself, so I don't understand my experiences. Could I be suffering from reincarnation or an extreme form of empathy?

My purpose in this book is not to convince anyone of the truth of reincarnation. I am simply telling the stories of people who, once they let go of their belief that the earth is flat, discovered uncharted territories in their life voyages.

CHAPTER 3

FROM WHERE THESE DREAMS?

THE COHEN FAMILY WAS HAVING A CHANUKAH PARTY in Holland, Pennsylvania, in 1987.[20] Audrey, thirty-two years old, and her brother Jay, thirty-one, as well as two other siblings, were there with their spouses and children. Growing up, Audrey and Jay had been inseparable, dubbed "Hansel and Gretel." Nothing, however, had prepared them for what was about to happen.

As Audrey recounted:

> Jay sits down at the piano, although he doesn't play piano. He starts to cry. Everyone gathers around and

---

20. Based on an interview with Audrey Cohen, March 23, 2017, corroborated by an interview with Jay Cohen. I also spoke with Audrey's ex-husband, who was not at the Chanukah party, but remembers Audrey telling him about it shortly afterwards.

asks what's the matter. He can't talk. Jay's wife asks what's wrong. She has never seen him cry. He says: "I just can't take it anymore. I can't do it one more night."

"What?" they ask him.

He starts to tell them about a nightmare he had almost every night when he was little and every few years since then. He'd had it again the night before the Chanukah party. I'm thinking it's very strange, because my bedroom was next to his. I had nightmares all the time, and he would sit with me and talk to me and make me laugh. But he never revealed any nightmares of his own.

He tells the story of the nightmare. He's about nine years old, and he lives in a wooden bungalow, poor, with soldiers outside the houses, in the court-yards. His parents are fighting. The father wants to leave and take the kids. The mother will not leave the house. "My kids were born in this house, and they will get married in this house."

His father protests, "Then our kids will die in this house. We have to leave." That's what they fight about.

They are a loving couple. The father makes peace with not leaving the house, but he teaches the boy what to do. The father has made a hole under the stove, and if the soldiers come, the boy should hide in that hole, or he should hide in the bed between the mattress and the springs.

His mother is pregnant and wants to have the baby in the house. Then the soldiers burst in, and there is no time for him to hide under the stove or in the bed. So his father takes him and throws him deep into the closet and closes the door. The boy can hear his father pleading with the soldiers, and he can hear his mother screaming.

Then the pleading and the screaming stop. He hears footsteps going toward the stove. He hears them overturn the stove. Then he hears them go into the bedroom. He hears the bed get turned over and put back. And then he hears the footsteps coming closer to the closet. They open the closet door and look in and feel around, but they don't find him. They close the door, and the footsteps go out. He hears screaming next door. Then the screaming gets fainter and fainter.

There is no sound in his home. He doesn't know what to do. His father told him to hide, but when is the hiding over? So he stays there for what seems like hours. Then he hears footsteps in his living room. They walk toward the stove. He hears the stove being moved. Then the footsteps run into the bedroom. He hears the bed go up and collapse down again. Then the footsteps approach the closet. The intruder opens the closet. Somebody is on top of him, grabbing him, and holding his eyes, like smothering him. Kicking and screaming, he is being dragged out of the closet.

When he is being dragged through the living room, the hand over his eyes slips somewhat. He sees his mother dead on the floor, her stomach slashed, and his father bloodied next to her, not moving.

At that moment, he freezes. He gets pulled outside, dragged down the steps, and dragged into a crowd of people. The people are all falling on top of him at the same time. Then he wakes up.

I approach him and say, "Do you know why you wake up at that point?"

He looks at me and says, "No."

Although our whole family is there, I see only my brother's eyes. I tell him my own nightmare, which I have had almost every night ever since I'm little. I live with my mother and my father and my twin brother. And my mother and father always fight about my father wanting to leave and my mother not wanting to hear about it. My father teaches me and my brother where to hide under the stove and in the bed. In the dream, which takes place on a Friday morning, I find my way out of the house and the village and through a fence into the forest. There's a non-Jewish boy, the son of a baker, who meets me there on Fridays and gives me two challahs to take to my family for Shabbat.

But this Friday morning, when the boy hands me the challahs, he looks at me and says, "You better get back to your village. There's trouble in the village. It's the soldiers."

I run so fast, with all my might, that I drop one challah, then the other. I see my brown shoes, running. That's how I know I'm a boy. I get through the fence. Very quietly I reach the bungalows, but everything is different. The soldiers are not where they usually are, and all the doors are open. I go up the steps to the porch of the six bungalows. I try not to look into anyone else's door.

I get to my house, and I go inside. That's when I see my mother, with her stomach sliced, and my father lying there motionless and bloodied. I have to find my twin. I run to the stove, hoping he'll be in our hiding place. It takes all my strength to push the stove, but he isn't there. I run into the bedroom. I grab the bed, and try to look up through the springs, but he isn't there. I think that the only place he could be is in the closet, so I open the closet. I call his name and feel around, but there is only silence and darkness. I go into the closet, and I find him. I try to pull him out, but he won't move. He's frozen in fear.

I'm the brave one, so I put my hands over his eyes and pull him out, because I know that if he sees what I am about to pull him past in the living room, he won't be able to live. So even though I'm pulling my own weight, I still do my best to keep my hands over his eyes. But when we pass my mother, I get weaker. My hand slips a little, and I know he sees, because his body turns as stiff as stone. Totally rigid.

I pull him out and pull him down the steps and try to get him to walk. I am trying to get him to the forest. But he isn't walking. Suddenly we are faced by soldiers. They get us. They put us with everyone else standing on the edge of this very long, deep ditch. At this point, my brother wakes up when the soldiers start to shoot. We all get shot and fall into the ditch, separately. There are at least three bodies between us. He is above me. He is not dead, but he was shot. I was not shot. I am lying wedged between bodies. I can't get to my brother, and I can't breathe. That's when I wake up every night.

When I finish my story, Jay gets up from the piano bench. We hug each other, and we cry and cry and cry. The rest of the family looks on, silent.

Dreams are the dispatch that lets most members of the Secret Society know that they belong. Most of their Holocaust dreams are recurrent, a dark apparition that haunts their nights again and again. Most such dreams begin at a young age, before the dreamer has ever seen a Holocaust movie or read a Holocaust book, or even before they became aware of the hell that ruled Europe in the mid-twentieth century.

One seven-year-old boy, born in 1943 in New York, had a recurrent dream that he was a boy with a different family. His family lay dead on the floor, shot by uniformed men wearing armbands with a strange symbol, "*x*'s with the ends broken back, like a pinwheel." Only when he was in sixth grade did he learn that the strange symbol was called a "swastika."

Jungian analyst and author of *Past Life Dreamwork* Dr. Sabine Lucas maintains that dreams are the most authentic proofs of a past life, as they descend spontaneously and directly from the person's superconscious. She explains how to determine when a dream is from a past life:

There are three types of past-life dreams: the classic type, the informatory type, and the hybrid type. The classic type is so different from other dreams that it can only be mistaken for something else if one is prejudiced, either by religious beliefs or by religiously followed dream theories. This type is lacking all normal dream features, such as familiar places and people, symbols, and arche-types. Instead, it is realistic and factual and has the déjà vu feeling of half-conscious memories. Often, it has the markings of a different century and cul-ture, and the dreamer may only be present as an observer on the scene.

The informatory type is even more unmistak-able, because it is completely devoid of images and actions. Instead, the dreamer is directly informed, or simply knows, that he or she was, for example, a revolutionary in Russia in 1918 who shot innocent people to death.

The hybrid type, which is the most common type, can be easily missed. If this were not so, and the other two types were more common, past-life dreams would have been included in psychologi-cal dream typologies a long time ago. The reason why this type is so difficult to recognize is that it combines realistic and symbolical elements.... Whenever I am not sure if I am dealing with ar-chetypal material or past-life material, I use the presence or absence of realistic and personalized elements as decisive criterion, because past-life material is personal, while archetypal material is universal and numinous.[21]

Dr. Lucas has devoted the last four decades to working with past-life dreams because she believes that if the issues or traumas that spark the dreams are not dealt with, they will continue to plague the person emotionally or even physically. One of my survey subjects illustrates the somatic effect in this life of past-life trauma. Martina Cockerel Gibson, a Christian woman born in Kentucky in 1958, dreamed:

> I know I was a Jewish woman, a bit heavyset with long, dark, curly hair. I was in a place, not my home, a place where we had been taken and put in rooms. Then some men came and got my two sons and took them away. I became a bit crazy. I would repeatedly ask the man, a small-boned man with a black beard, when were they going to bring my children back. I knew that asking him this question was hurting him, but I had to ask. I kept asking. I know these children. I can see them in my mind like it is a picture. They are about four and six. I see them in the picture side by side wearing little hats. They are mine....
>
> Later, we have been moved. I am in a line with other women. Then I am shot in the back and fall face forward into a trench. I am facing to my left on my stomach. I can't move my arms. I really want to move my arms to push myself up to breath better.

---

21. Sabine Lucas, PhD, *Past Life Dreamwork: Healing the Soul through Understanding Karmic Patterns* (Rochester, Vermont: Bear and Company, 2008), pp. 18–19.

Something is on top of me, blocking out part of the light. Then it is over.

As a child, I used to wake up at night with a stabbing pain between my shoulder blades. It was so bad that I would have to stiffen my back and arch up to stop the pain. I still can't stand to be in a position where I can't move my arms. I can't stand to feel like I can't move, such as being in a tight coat. I have to sleep with a fan blowing on me to keep the air flowing.

A past life in the Holocaust appears in one's dreams like an unexpected and unwelcome visitor. Upon waking (or perhaps years later), one may want to decipher the identity of the visitor. Although the dreamer fully understands that "that was me," she may seek to know more about who she was then or to corroborate her dream with historical facts.

A Christian woman from Wisconsin who was born in 1960 wrote to me:

I never thought there were others like myself out there. I never met anyone else who has had the experiences I've had. To my relief, here you are! This is my story:

At the age of four I began to have nightmares. But in them I was a grown woman. They were always about running through an unfamiliar city, but one very unlike the one I lived in. The streets and alleys were of brick or cobblestone, the houses smaller and much further apart than the ones I knew in waking life. It seemed an endless rush through this town, being pursued by a hulking figure whom I called Billy (don't ask me why that name, I do not know!). Every place I found to hide, there were already people there, hissing, "No room, we are already too many! Find somewhere else!"

As I grew older, "Billy" was replaced by soldiers. They were always right at my heels, and the sense of panic was overwhelming. In the dreams, I've hidden in barn lofts, attics, behind piles of trash in alleys.

I would see a stream of people crossing an iron trestle, like a bridge, that stretched over an underpass that could be walked or driven through. I would stand there and watch with horror as unclothed, bleeding masses of people were herded across the bridge, blood dripping to the pavement below. In the next moment, I was stopped by soldiers who demanded my jewelry, my wedding ring. They then chased me through a field, held me down, and slit my throat. I could actually feel my soul leave my body, quite literally, through the wound. Then I would wake up. These nightmares persisted into my adulthood.

I've read as many survivors' stories as I can get my hands on since then, and the nightmares completely stopped. I studied the pictures, wondering if one day I would find a picture of that train trestle. I read one account by [Holocaust survivor] Livia Bitton-Jackson (*I Have Lived a Thousand Years*), where the people of her town were ordered to march across a bridge by a train station, stripped of their clothing and belongings. As I read, I was utterly awash with what I can only describe as a feeling of familiarity, of, "Yes, this is it, this is what happened!" This has been the only instance of overwhelming recognition that I've encountered.

While to me it was an astounding find, I would still believe, even without this seeming corroborating evidence, that I was there in a former life. No other explanation makes sense to me. There is no way a four-year-old in 1964 would have the kind of information necessary to inspire such awful dreams.

A woman born to a Christian family in Australia in 1966 had a dream of a concentration camp that she considered "stupid" until she accidently found corroboration many years later.

I dreamed of a place that was being built. There was a lot of mud, and they seemed to be digging a lap pool. Myself and Joseph (I knew him in the dream, and we spoke a language that I understood in the dream but not awake) got out of a covered truck along with many others. I saw a woman and her two girls get out of a staff car, and one stumbled. I immediately went to help and ended up as a tutor/ nanny but inevitably was gassed. I thought it was stupid. Whoever had heard of a lap pool in a concentration camp?

Years later, when the Internet was born, I was on a website about Auschwitz and, scrolling through, there was a picture of the lap pool!

Dr. Sabine Lucas herself had a Holocaust-era dream and was able to corroborate some of the details. The dream, which she had in her seventies, was the "informatory type" of dream that she defines above as "devoid of images and actions. Instead, the dreamer is directly informed, or simply knows...." Dr. Lucas refers to such direct receiving of information as a "download."

The first thing I saw in the dream was a white delivery van, which was parked in front of a Jewish cemetery. Then I received a download of information, most of which I remembered when I awoke. The year was 1936, and the cemetery where the van was parked was located in Tuebingen, in southern Germany. A young Jewish woman lawyer named Hannah Wolpert had been arrested by the Gestapo for being a member or the founder of a local organization. In the dream I knew the name of the organization but remembered only fragments of it when I awoke. Hannah Wolpert had held the position of an assistant in the Law Department of Tuebingen University before all Jewish state employees were forced into retirement. She was married to a non-Jew, which for racial reasons was frowned upon by the Nazis.

In my dream I was aware of a negative turn of events that had occurred the year before, which had precipitated Hannah's arrest. Only later did

I find out that this had been the passage of the notorious Nuremberg Laws in 1935, which had imposed severe restrictions on the Jewish population. According to these laws, Jews were prohibited from marrying non-Jews.... In addition, Jews were no longer allowed to hold public office or study at German universities.

Hannah was apparently in conflict with one of these new laws, because after being cross-examined by the Gestapo she was loaded into the white delivery van and driven to the Jewish cemetery, where she was executed by a shot in the back of her neck. Her body was then dumped inside the entrance of the cemetery.

When I woke up, I felt a sharp pain in the back of my neck, as if I were Hannah Wolpert myself.[22]

Dr. Lucas, who was born in Germany, looked for corroboration of her dream. Although she didn't recognize Wolpert as a Jewish name, a Google search taught her otherwise. While "Wolpert" is not exclusively Jewish, it is of Ashkenazi origins, and the area of Germany where the name is most common corresponds to the state where Tuebingen is located. She also discovered academic connections between the Wolpert family and Tuebingen University.

In an email correspondence with me, Dr. Lucas wrote:

The synagogue in Tuebingen was burned down by the Nazis, and probably all documents were

---

22. From the documentary film *A Row of Tombs: Jung and Reincarnation.*

destroyed. I doubt that Tuebingen University, which was completely infiltrated by the Nazis and their propaganda, kept any records of Jewish members of staff. So why travel to Tuebingen for that purpose? ... But the little I was able to verify of the information I received in my dream was pretty astounding even without that. The geographical location of the name "Wolpert" in the Tuebingen area, the connection between surviving members of the Wolpert family and the university, the timeline of the interrogation and execution in relationship to the passing of the Nuremberg Laws and even the white delivery van where Hannah's execution took place.

By some miracle, I found the same white van online on a website displaying old car models. It was described as a Citroën, which was built in the thirties and was used by the Nazis for unknown purposes. It usually bore the inscription "medical supplies" or some other cover-up of that nature.[23]

Sometimes corroboration comes without seeking it. Anna is the regional administrator of a large American NGO. She was born in 1957 in St. Louis to a Jewish family with no direct link to the Holocaust. When Anna was five years old, she

---

23. In 1936, Sabine Lucas was three years old, an only child living with her parents in Berlin. Therefore, as the mature adult having this dream, she concluded that she could not have been a reincarnation of Hannah Wolpert, but rather a "sister soul" or a simultaneous incarnation where a soul splits into two bodies in order to accomplish different missions. Kabbalah would account for the phenomenon with the concept of *ibbur*, where a soul that leaves a body upon death can enter another body in order to help that person or for its own agenda.

began to have a recurring dream that she was being tortured in a laboratory setting. Her torturers were a doctor wearing a white coat and, incongruously, a man in a military uniform. She had this recurring dream until she was ten years old.

When she later learned about the Holocaust, Anna intuited, "The Nazis were the people in my dream." Starting in third grade, she became obsessed with the subject, reading whatever Holocaust books and seeing whatever Holocaust movies were available at that time. At some point, she concluded that she had been experimented upon in Dr. Josef Mengele's infamous twin experiments in Auschwitz.

Years later, Anna was invited for a Shabbat meal in New York City. When she arrived, an elderly gentleman who was a fellow guest opened the door for her. She looked at him quizzically. She knew him, but she couldn't place from where. He also stared at her with a perplexed recognition. Finally, still standing at the doorway, he said, "I think I know you." Anna replied, "I think I know you, too." Neither of them, however, could figure out from where.

The connection between Anna and this man, many decades older than she, was so strong that the man's wife started to get upset. The man and his wife had been guests in this home many times before, and it was known that he was a survivor of the Holocaust. Over Shabbat lunch, however, the elderly man revealed something that his hosts had never before heard: He had been a subject in the Mengele twin experiments.

Since very young children do not read graphic Holocaust books nor see Holocaust movies, their dreams of Holocaust images would seem to corroborate that their dreams issue from a past life, or what I call NORE (No Other Rational Explanation). One of my subjects related that when she was a child, she walked into the living room while her mother was watching a Holocaust film, and her mother made her leave the room. Typically, parents do not allow their young children to be exposed to such images. Thus, the dream of a young Los Angeles–born girl is particularly chilling:

> When I was about nine or ten, I was sick with a fever. I had a dream in which I was tossed into a pile of bodies and was too weak to move. More bodies were put on top of me, and, after being unable to move from under them, my soul left my body.

Feverish prisoners being tossed onto piles of bodies when they were not yet dead was a common occurrence in the concentration camps. NORE.

A girl born to a Christian family in 1950 in Englewood, California, had a similarly horrific dream. At the age of ten, never having heard of the Einsatzgruppen, the Nazi mobile killing squads that shot Jews lined up along pits, she dreamed that she was lying next to her mother in a huge hole or pit. She looked up and saw a bulldozer at the edge of the pit, dumping dirt on them to cover them up. Many decades later, she still recalled that nightmare. "It felt so real," she insists, "as if I was reliving it." NORE.

Junie Maggio was born into a Roman Catholic family in Kansas City, Missouri, in 1952. At the age of five or six, Junie had a nightmare of a situation that we now know happened regularly during the Holocaust:

> I dreamed I was in the back of a truck with an adult and a few children, and we were covered with potatoes—mounds of potatoes. It was nighttime. The driver of the potato truck assumed he was going to be waved through the checkpoint, which was a road leading into a dense forest. The German guard sneered and ordered him to stop and get out of the truck and walk with him to the back of it. He made the driver watch as he smilingly machine-gunned into the potatoes. The machine-gun fire struck a child, but the adult covered the mouth of the child so they would not yell out. It seemed like that child was me.
>
> The guard waited and then motioned for the driver to get into the truck and go on. After that I just seemed to disappear. I recall I woke up screaming about it. My mom ran into my room. I exclaimed about Hitler, Nazis, and so on, and she tried to reassure me that they were all dead and gone.
>
> As I got older, I believed this must have been from a scene in some movie. I have been trying to find a World War II movie with such a scene in the story line as I described. I think it would have to be a film that focused on the resistance in Poland or somewhere else in Eastern Europe, a movie that was out before 1958. But my research has not found such a movie.

Of course, some children's dreams with historically accurate content could be accounted for by epigenetics, the concept that traumas can be passed down genetically from parents to children. The experiments of epigenetic scientists Dr. Siddhartha Mukherjee and Dr. Rachel Yehuda have demonstrated how epigenetic changes in a parents' genes, such as stress characteristics, are passed down to their children as biological information.

Susan had a grandmother named Reeva who survived Auschwitz. Years after her grandmother died, Susan named her daughter Reeva after this grandmother.

> When my daughter Reeva was a toddler, she had extremely vivid dreams, but she didn't find them scary. She would tell me that she had a dream that all the mommies had to go to one side and all the daddies to the other side (and more details that I can't recall now but were clearly a very vivid description of what may have occurred when the trains arrived at Auschwitz).
>
> Another dream she had was that "we were all pushed into a small room and it was so squishy and then big men were squirting something from sticks [sounded like she was describing guns, but she probably didn't know that word at that point and had never seen one] and everyone was falling down and my knee hurt so much and the floor was so sticky when I was on the floor...."
>
> I asked her what was on the floor, and she said, "I don't know, maybe bubble gum?"

I do not know whether epigenetics could account for such specific dream content, but in order to rule out this possibility, my survey asked whether parents or grandparents were Holocaust survivors. Except for four cases where I specifically note that the survey respondent is the child or grandchild of survivors, I have chosen not to use the testimony of such respondents because their dreams, flashbacks, or phobias may have been inherited biologically or suggested by what they heard in their homes. I preface almost all of the accounts by noting the religion in which the respondent was raised because Christian children are less likely to have been exposed to any discussion of the Holocaust. Unless otherwise noted, all Jewish-born respondents came from families that had no direct connection to the Holocaust, meaning close relatives who perished or survived.

Although psychologists explain that recurring dreams are a message from the subconscious about unresolved issues and traumas that have not been worked through, the subconscious is usually cautious about what it reveals. In the following case, the dreamer woke herself up rather than view a horrific memory.

Sheila Segall, born in Chicago in 1963 to a Jewish family, had three dreams that recurred from the age of three until the age of twelve:

> In one dream, I saw me from outside of myself. I had very short hair and looked like a boy. I saw a ticking bomb in a barrel-like object that I was crouching behind, trying to hide. I felt a sharp pain in my chest.

My face contorted in pain as I was hurled across what appeared to be blue wooden shelves. Then I woke up.

In another dream, I saw a doctor and soldiers in a room with a table and machines in it. I was tied down. When I had this dream, I would wake myself up, as I did not want to see the rest.

In another dream, I saw a lot of smoke and wooden buildings. There was a truck filled with dead bodies.

All of these dreams started before I had words to describe them. We did not discuss the Holocaust much growing up. In fact, I actually had an aversion to learning anything related to it. I would avoid the subject. When I was fourteen and saw my first documentary about the Holocaust, I actually threw up while watching and started hyperventilating.

When someone told me about a Holocaust survivor who was going on a March of the Living in Poland, I said to this person without thinking, "I never want to go back there." I got very emotional and said, "They can go back because they survived. I didn't, so I am not going back."

I don't know where that reaction came from, as someone who was born in Chicago and was never in Europe.

While Sheila woke herself up rather than view a horrific scene, some people deliberately choose to see more than the initial boundaries of their dream. This is illustrated by a case related to me by Judy Tashbook Safern. When Judy lived in Jerusalem in the 1990s, she met a woman who was a gifted seamstress.

> She had terrible anxiety and PTSD, but could not pinpoint the source until she began remembering and piecing together fragments of dreams. She had recurring, detailed dreams in which she was forced to sit at a sewing machine and felt terror all around her. Once she became insistent enough and drew enough courage, she began trying to enlarge the scope of her dreams, look around while in them, and remember what she saw and experienced in the dreams. She came to realize that she was a re-incarnation of a young girl who, before her murder, had been enslaved in a workroom, sewing concen-tration camp uniforms.

Dr. Sarah Levy was born into a Jewish family in New York in 1972. Her maternal grandparents did discuss the Holocaust when she was growing up. Since as early as she can remember, she has had a recurring dream of "Nazis trying to break down my door while I try to find a place to hide." Although this could be dismissed as a simple anxiety dream of childhood, the dream has pursued her into adulthood. Even now, with a PhD in Neuropsychology and as an associate professor at the CUNY Graduate Center who has published peer-reviewed research in scientific journals, Dr. Levy still sporadically has this dream.

The more distant the person is from any exposure to the subject of the Holocaust, the more likely the dreams come from a past-life experience. Sonia Gregory was born into a Methodist family in Sheffield, England, in 1948, long before Holocaust movies and memoirs were available. She had a recurrent dream from a young age until she was "almost a teenager." In the dream, she and another woman, "not my mother, an aunt perhaps," were digging a pit. Only at the last minute, before she was shot, did she realize that she was digging her own grave.

Sometimes the person having the dream is torn between the conviction that the dream must be a past-life experience and the taboo of believing in reincarnation. For example, a devout Protestant woman born in Greenville, Alabama, in 1942, wrote to me:

> I don't think any of us knew anything about the Holocaust.... I have been going through my old journals and have found a dream that seems to be connected to the Holocaust. The entry was dated July 3, 2001.
>
> In the dream I was working in a government agency. I was told that it was necessary to locate the "children of the name-change men." I knew these men had been arrested, but their families had not. Although I was assured that no harm would come to them, I didn't believe it.
>
> The scene changes, and I am in a home with a mother, her small son, and daughter. I know this is a family of a "name-change man." While I try to convince the woman to take her children and flee,

people arrive in front of the house. I tell the woman we must escape through the windows at the back of the house. The dream ends.

In trying to make sense of this dream, I have come to the conclusion that the place was Germany, probably Munich, during the 1930s. I have not found any reference to "name-change men" but wonder if it could be a reference to a group who made counterfeit papers for Jews to either escape or to find work.

I assume that there is a reason for my dreams. I have no idea what I'm supposed to do with them. I have come to believe that they are fragments of a past life as a Jewish woman. The official verdict of my religion, Christianity, would be that my belief that I had lived before would be a heresy. Unofficially, many Christians would not think that.

Victoria Thompson was born into a Catholic family in Adelaide, Australia, in 1979.

I have had dreams [of the Holocaust] for as long as I can remember, as well as a fascination with World War II and the Jews/Nazis.

I am a fourth-generation Australian Catholic with no known connection to these events. It was not a topic of discussion in our household, and I don't remember reading or hearing anything much about it before the dreams started.

The dreams are always similar and a variation on the same theme. I am in a lineup of women, and we are being "sorted" and herded. Sometimes it's very confused and frantic…sometimes silent and drawn out… Sometimes we are standing silently in a queue, but there is always a feeling of dread, fear, and inevitability…like I am waiting to die or be killed.

Reincarnation generally goes against Christian beliefs and scientific ones, but these dreams do leave me wondering.

Most people do not have dreams and flashbacks of a past life because the partition between lives is usually solid and firm. Two reasons can account for the ruptures in the partition recounted in this book.

First, there can be many years or centuries between incarnations, but when people come back quickly, the partition is more like a thin veil than a wall. Esteemed author and psychologist Dr. Miriam Adahan was born to a Jewish family in Detroit in 1942. From the age of three she had nightmares about Nazis, as well as phobias of striped pajamas and German shepherd dogs. At the age of twenty-eight, she went to a Kabbalist, who told her that she came to this lifetime directly from the Holocaust, without any rest period in between, and that was the reason she had the "bleed-through" from a previous lifetime. He told her that she had to make a firm separation by looking forward, not backward.

The second reason that people may be haunted by a previous lifetime is if they experienced a traumatic death. In

Professor Ian Stevenson's research of thousands of cases of children who spoke about their previous life, most of them had experienced an "unnatural" death, either by an accident, a murder, or other such causes. (The rest are children who reported having died of illness as a young child, and were reborn to the same family a few years later.)

Both these reasons may account for the nightmares, flashbacks, phobias, and panic attacks reported in this book. Most of my survey respondents were born within a decade and a half of the Holocaust. The rest were born less than fifty years after their purported deaths, attenuated time periods that allowed the soul little "between-life" respite to process and integrate their previous experiences. Also, whether they were murdered by the genocidal machinations of the Nazis, were killed as soldiers, or committed suicide, all of them died violent deaths.

Dr. Philip E. Miller was born in 1945 in Providence, Rhode Island, to a Jewish family. He had a recurring dream that started when he was just three years old (as supported by the fact that his family moved out of that house before his fourth birthday). The dream recurred periodically until Dr. Miller was sixty-seven, when the dream appeared with many more details—and a resolution.

> As a preschooler, I remember awakening, screaming, after having seen a field of dead bodies. Not once, but often. Over the years, parents, teachers, and doctors told me that I had an overactive imagination.
>
> About three years ago, I dreamed I was walking in single file with other partisans through woods and fields. The man behind me was chanting something

in a whisper. We came out of the woods into a field
filled with dead bodies. There was no way to know if
they were Jews or gentiles. Perhaps they were residents of a peasant village murdered by the Germans
or the Russians.

At that point, at the age of sixty-seven, Dr. Miller realized
that the man behind him in his dream was chanting verses of
Tehillim (Psalms). Once he recognized this sacred compo-
nent, the dream never recurred.

In virtually all cases, the child having the dream has no
idea that it is connected to the Holocaust; only later, upon
learning of the Holocaust, does he or she connect the horrific
dream to that historic event. Thus, Adina Hershberg, who
was born in 1957 in Wilkes-Barre, Pennsylvania, to a Jewish
family, could not understand the source of her dreams until
adulthood. When she was eight years old, she started having
dreams about hiding so that "the evil people" would not find
her.

"I started having the nightmares years before I learned
of the Holocaust. I guess that later, after reading about the
Holocaust and seeing films about it, I felt that the reasons I
had such nightmares about hiding in different places is that I
had lived in that time."

The nightmares lasted until Adina was in her forties,
with her still having no idea that she might have a deeper
connection to the content of her dreams. Then a close friend
"told me that she had gone to a Kabbalist, who said that she
was a reincarnation of someone who had been killed in the

Holocaust. When she told me that, I felt deeply that I am as well." In the wake of that corroboration, Adina's nightmares stopped.

For Mary Beth Harris, born into a Protestant family in San Diego in 1962, it took many years to connect her childhood nightmares and strange bedtime fears with the Holocaust. From the age of three, throughout her childhood and into her adulthood, Mary Beth dreamed of running and hiding in woods or the basements of apartment buildings. In some of her dreams, she was cold and hungry.

> As a young child, when a siren would go off in the middle of the night, I thought it was black ginger-bread men coming in droves to get us. I now realize [these "gingerbread men"] were soldiers.

Mary Beth's sister, born in 1959, shared her fears of being snatched away. In order to be prepared for the worst, the two children shared a touching bedtime ritual described by Mary Beth:

> We packed a bag every night with our most im-portant possessions in it, which was our Bible, our stuffed animals, and toothbrushes and hairbrush-es. We would go to bed sucking our thumbs, facing each other with our pinkies hooked so that we would not get separated if the "soldiers" came.
>
> When I got into my twenties and began reading books about [the Holocaust], I was obsessed with it. It has only been in the past couple of years, since I started believing in reincarnation, that I began to

draw the connection. As adults, my sister and I realized we had the same type of dreams.

So terrifying were Mary Beth's fears of being taken by the "black gingerbread men/soldiers" that she could not sleep alone until she was nearly an adult. As a smaller child, she crawled into bed with her parents, and as she got older, with her siblings.

A strange addendum to Mary Beth's account is the story of her younger brother Chuck:

He was the first boy after five girls, with a five-year break in kids. At two years old, he would dress like a soldier (though my dad was long out of the Navy and didn't talk about it) and circle the house to protect the family. Through his life, he has stocked weapons, gas masks, and nearly everything he would need for his family (us) to survive, should we need to hide out.

He has been so obsessed with protecting all of us, including our youngest brother and now all the nieces and nephews, that it almost seems he has put living what could have been his best life on hold. My sister (the one I hooked pinkie fingers with) said that she remembers a day when my brother was around two years old that she said, "Oh good! Chuck's here! He will take care of us now!" And she was able to relax a little.

I wonder if we may have been Chuck's children or had some type of connection to him and he lost his family and those he loved in that time, because he seems to have always had a great need to protect everyone else at his own expense. I have almost sensed guilt or a sense of duty that he is trying to make up for. Now that I have given reincarnation a thought, this all makes a lot of sense.

Both Dr. Brian Weiss and Dr. Ian Stevenson came to believe that certain phobias, anxieties, and panic attacks of their patients could not be explained—or treated—without the background of past lives. An example of how past-life dreams in childhood can haunt a person into adulthood and even become more frightening is Angela Lopez. She was born in 1966 in Brooklyn to a Catholic family, her mother Italian and her father Puerto Rican. She started having dreams connected to the Holocaust when she was five or six years old.

> In the earliest dream that I recall, I see barbed-wire fences and military. I am a girl, a prisoner, and there are many of us. We are all standing in line on soil ground. I feel afraid. The dream was always like that, the same thing over and over throughout the years.

Then, one night in 2014, at the age of forty-eight, Angela's recurrent dream "escalated":

> I never felt so afraid for my life as I did in that dream last night. Last night I was in a building without windows, and one soldier was looking at me with a wicked smile. I knew I was a sitting duck, and that they had control over my life. I was at their mercy.

The inhumanity exhibited was so frightening, I felt so trapped, I couldn't believe I was really there and that this was really happening. I tried to tell myself this was just a dream, but I wouldn't believe myself. "This *is* real," my dream self was telling my real self.

My turn was coming, and I was so afraid. I was absolutely horrified by them, by their indifference. I could tell by the uniforms they were Nazis. I am not Jewish, nor am I German, but in these recurring dreams I am a Jewish girl. And what I feel in these dreams exceeds my capacity to fully capture in words.

For the first time yesterday, I experienced a panic attack due to the nightmare. I woke up with a racing heart, and it wouldn't stop until several hours later. I didn't fully relax until the evening, when I finally cried to let it out.

The next day Angela googled "past-life Holocaust dreams" and found me. She ended her email to me, "Just thought I would share. I am not a true believer in reincarnation, but this dream is always so vivid and real."

Just as very young children dreaming about experiences they were not exposed to in this lifetime may point to reincarnation, so may xenoglossy, dreaming in a foreign language. The term *xenoglossy* was coined by French parapsychologist Charles Richet in 1905, and is defined as the putative paranormal phenomenon in which a person is able to speak or write a language he or she could not have acquired by natural means.

Laurie Sussman was born in Brooklyn, New York, in 1953, to a Jewish family. As a child, she dreamed of the Holocaust, but she does not remember the content of those dreams. However, in 2017, she had two "remarkable yet frightening dreams."

> In the first, I was in Poland during the Shoah. I was running from the Nazis, and I spoke and understood perfect Polish. I have never heard Polish or lived near people who spoke Polish. I never visited Poland, and in truth, I am afraid to go to Poland or anywhere else in Europe, especially countries that came under the influence of the Nazis during the Shoah. I am absolutely terrified of even being near the people of those countries, especially Germany and Poland.

> The second dream, which I had several weeks later, took place in Israel in the late 1940s. In that dream, I spoke fluent German and Hebrew. There was an old man with horn-rimmed glasses walking down a flight of stairs leading to the outside area of a museum of some kind in Israel. The dream had to do with chasing down and killing a Nazi or collaborator who was hurting Jewish children. The man's face was extremely familiar.

> Also, I should mention that on my first trip to Israel in 1972, we went to visit the Holocaust museum at Kibbutz Lohamei HaGeta'ot. Upon viewing one of the photos there, I started crying

hysterically and almost fainted. The guide had to lead me out.

I am extremely claustrophobic. I am terrified of being on a crowded train without a seat. When I was in my mid-twenties and newly married, I was on the subway coming home from work in Manhattan to meet my husband near my parents' home in Brooklyn. The train got stuck in the tunnel. I was standing with crowds of others, all packed in like sardines. I panicked and was trying not to cry. I kept thinking that I was on a train going to Auschwitz.

Daria was born in Camden, New Jersey, in 1970 to a family of Ukrainian Byzantine Catholics. As a child, she had a recurring dream of being a boy playing behind a wooden schoolhouse with aircraft flying overhead and sirens. As an adult, she has dreamed in Hebrew and German, languages she never learned. "I had dreams where I read and spoke German. I would wake up with the German word in my head and look it up, and it was real."

She also dreamed of several rabbis dressed in black surrounding her in a circle and chanting in Hebrew. When growing up, she was claustrophobic and feared smokestacks and gas ovens. But the most remarkable "evidence" of her past life in the Holocaust is something that would have bolstered the hypotheses of Professor Ian Stevenson.

Professor Stevenson's magnum opus, *Reincarnation and Biology: A Contribution to the Etiology of Birthmarks and Birth*

Defects,[24] is a 2,268-page, two-volume work that connects birthmarks and physical anomalies in the children he studied with the wounds and physical markings of their purported past-life personalities, which in some cases were confirmed by the dead person's autopsy record and photos. For example, one child who reported that he had been shot to death from the back had a small circular birthmark at the back of his head. Professor Stevenson surmised that if the bullet had entered his head at that point, it must have come out through his skull in the front of his head. Professor Stevenson brushed aside the child's hair and found on his scalp a second round birthmark.

Daria, the Ukrainian Byzantine woman mentioned above, has a birthmark on her inner left forearm that is clearly six characters and about four inches long, strangely reminiscent of the tattooed numbers with which concentration camp prisoners were branded.

A woman born in America in 1962 to a Christian family sent me an email with this eerie story:

> The Holocaust was something I knew little about growing up. My father was in the US Army during World War II. He told me the Germans were horrible people and had done awful things to people in Europe, but he was never specific.

---

24. Westport, CT: Praeger, 1997.

At the age of seventeen, I started having nightmares about being crowded into a small, dimly lit room with many other women. There would be the sounds of screaming, panic, gasping, and choking [an apt description of the gas chambers]. I would be clawing at the walls, trying to escape, and then wake up with my heart pounding. It would be hard to fall back asleep.

Another odd experience came in the late 1970s, when my father began to purchase big band records out of nostalgia for the '40s. Although I had never heard many of these songs, I quickly picked up on many of the lyrics as if I already knew them and seemed to be recalling them. It was an eerie feeling.

Not long after, my dreams began to expand to being on a stage, singing, in a dimly lit, smoky Parisian-type nightclub with a small dance floor in front of me and a balcony seating area with tables and chairs beyond the dance floor.

After singing, I would go into this area and visit with the people sitting there. Some of the men were in gray uniforms with swastikas. I would feel an odd sense of revulsion as I tried to be friendly towards them. My husband revealed to me that a few times he could tell I was having some kind of dream because I was singing in French and then started chattering away in French. Other than a few rudimentary phrases and words remembered from high school French class, I don't speak French all that well.

The scariest dreams have been of being hustled out of a nightclub by two men. I am trying to escape their grips on my arms and get away from them. There is a big black car curbside. The door opens, and a man in an officer's uniform is sitting in the back seat with a little blond-haired boy of about five or six years of age. I feel the bottom drop out of my stomach and stop resisting the two men. The man quietly tells me to get in the car, and I do. The car pulls into a huge place with many buildings. I get out of the car, and the little boy is pulled away from me and we are placed in opposite lines. I am crying and begging the people in uniform to let me have my son.

In an odd real-life experience, I became acquainted seven years back with a woman who, like myself, was a high school art teacher. Malgorzata (who immigrated to this country from Poland after the fall of Communism there) and I seemed to hit it off. There was always this feeling of déjà vu with her, but I never mentioned it because I didn't want to seem weird. One day she asked me if it ever seemed to me as if we had known each other before, as if from a long time ago. I was floored! I said, yes, it did.

She smiled slyly and said, "Perhaps in another life? Yes?" I asked her if she wanted to talk further about it, and she said, "No, not now. Perhaps another time." The subject was never brought up again.

When Holocaust dreams occur to an adult, there is usually an obvious trigger. As Dr. Sabine Lucas wrote: "Dreams were triggered either by a similarity of past and present events, or by a visit to a past-life locale, or by a need to access past-life knowledge."[25] For example, several of my subjects testified that their dreams began when they were pregnant or after the birth of their first child, and their dreams were filled with the fear of losing a child.

Cindy Lanzbom's recurring dream started when she was twenty-seven and lasted throughout her pregnancy with her second child. She would hear SS Stormtroopers' boots stomping down the hallway, and she feared they were coming for her older daughter. Throughout the pregnancy, she also had a fear that someone was coming up behind her and hitting her over the head. Both the dreams and the phobia disappeared upon the birth of her second child. However, she adds, "But my obsession with the Holocaust has only intensified with the passing years."

A scientist born in America in 1983 had a single frightening dream at the age of twenty-seven, three days after the birth of her son.

> I felt cold. I smelled the smells. The smell of mud. There was a little snow. We were dressed inappropriately for the cold. I was holding my baby, I don't know if a boy or a girl, in a yellow outfit. I was worried because the outfit was not warm enough. I was the adult responsible for someone else too. There was mud everywhere. We came to a place with barbed wire, and there was a line.

---

25. *Past Life Dreamwork*, p. 240.

A Nazi soldier grabbed my baby from me. I woke up crying. There was no purpose for my life anymore if my child was taken away from me....

All my life, I knew I would be a mother. I wasn't dreaming about a wedding, I was always dreaming about having a child.

Adina S., who grew up in an Orthodox Jewish family in America in the '70s, was exposed throughout her school years to many Holocaust books and movies, but her nightmares of the Holocaust did not begin until after the birth of her first son. After each of her four children was born, she suffered postpartum depression and had a period of dreaming of the Holocaust.

Every time my kids were sick when they were toddlers and they were feverish, I would have nightmares that I did not have medicine for them and that they were suffering and I could not do anything about it. I feel as if I lost a young child in the Warsaw Ghetto to illness from starvation. I am tearing up as I write this.

I have spoken to a psychologist about this, and she said that this comes up in therapy for many people, the sense that they were there in the Holocaust.

My children are older now, and the feelings are not so intense. I was once explaining to my friend why I did not have more children after my fourth, since large families are common in my circles. I told her, "I can't do it again. I cannot go back and relive the Holocaust." This sounds so crazy as I am writing this.

For Sandy Erez, born in Brooklyn in 1959 to a Jewish family, the trigger of her nightmares was totally unexpected. In Hebrew school at the age of eight, she learned to say the Shema, the profession of Jewish faith that is recited every morning and evening in the Jewish liturgy, as well as at bedtime, and also at the time of death. Her teacher instructed the children to say the Shema at night with one of their parents. So that night eight-year-old Sandy recited the Shema with her father. "It was a very auspicious and memorable moment," she recounts. "The image is still very fresh in my head."

But that night Sandy had a traumatic dream:

> I was a child on a cold concrete floor, crawling on my stomach, and it was raining. There were people screaming. I was being whipped on my back. The pain was intense. Experts say you cannot feel pain in your dreams. I very, very, very much remember the pain, across the bottom of my back, and being terrified.
>
> For years after that I have had that same dream, some only with fingers digging into my back (all with pain so real I would check my back in a mirror when I woke up), or being whipped. The dreams continued for years and years. I even went to a psychologist at age ten because I would wake up screaming nightly.
>
> Eventually the dreams abated...but I still have some pieces of them sometimes, especially stinging pain across my back and me trying to pry fingers off of me.

Sandy's dream correlates with descriptions from the few surviving Sonderkommandos, who removed the corpses from the gas chambers. When the Zyklon B gas was released and the victims started gasping for air and collapsing on the concrete floor, many of them panicked and climbed on top of each other, desperately clawing to get to the door, which was, of course, sealed, or to get higher, since the heavy gas sank. Most of the Jews, realizing that death was imminent, called out the Shema. Thus, reciting the Shema for the first time, little Sandy's Holocaust memory of her back being clawed was triggered. The "rain" she dreamed of was the Zyklon B gas misting from above.

For Cathy R., the trigger of her dreams was her conversion to Judaism at the age of twenty-one. Born in 1988 in Seattle to two evangelical pastors, Cathy was raised Christian.

> About a month after I converted, I had really strong, vivid dreams about the Holocaust. One night my brother had to wake me up because I was crying and yelling, "Not another Holocaust!" in my sleep.
>
> In one dream, I remember being taken as a girl around the age of sixteen or eighteen into an underground facility below a place that had barracks and holding areas aboveground. A Nazi doctor was talking to me, asking questions about my family background. I remember being strapped to a wooden chair with two leather bands. Then he injected me more than once, and things became very blurry and muffled.
>
> Right before I was awakened by my family, I remember being taken to the room with the wooden

chair again and getting the impression that I was too old for what they needed. Then the searing pain of numbers being burned into my arm, and I was screaming and crying, "Not another Holocaust." My arm was tingling for days with the ghost-like feeling of numbers being there.

Another convert to Judaism from a Christian family was born in Oregon in 1952. As a young child, she had a recurring dream about a pit of fire. In 1944 in Auschwitz and other death camps, when the influx of Hungarian Jews overwhelmed the capacity of the gas chambers and crematoria, the Germans developed an efficient shortcut. They had prisoners dig deep and long pits, into which they put logs, which they set afire. Then they shot their victims, who would fall into the flames, achieving murder and cremation simultaneously. Since many times the shots missed, many victims were burned alive in the pits.

This would seem to be the background of this child's dreams:

Almost every night from at age four until about age twelve, I would dream that my whole family and all my friends were in a pit of fire screaming and crying. I had a swing from the playground that I held in my two hands on its long chains, and I was told that I could choose two people to save and fly away with them to safety. I couldn't decide! How do you decide? My brother and mother? My father and mother? My best friend and sister?! It was an impossible decision, so I dropped the swing and fell down into the pit with everyone. I would wake up shivering and crying and run to my parents' room. I never told them what the dream was.

I could never choose teammates for softball or red rover and hated playing musical chairs and the farmer in the dell. I refused to play any game of choosing, which often irritated my teacher.

Laura Shulman was born to a Christian family in Iowa in 1951. From the age of thirteen she told her parents that she was really Jewish, and eventually converted to Judaism as an adult. She describes a strange (and unique) revelation connected to her Holocaust dreams:

I've had several powerful dreams that felt like something beyond regular dreams. One has haunted me—I watched a young woman I didn't know in different black and white vignettes. I could see her clearly—olive skin, dark hair, short and stocky. She was sent to Canada to train to be a spy. Later, she was caught in Germany. She was led to a stone wall. I knew she would be shot. Then I heard a beautifully modulated woman's voice loud in my head saying, "That woman is you." I woke with a start.

As might be expected, dreams of the gas chambers have occurred to several of my subjects. A woman born in Boston in 1970 to a Jewish family had a recurring dream that started when she was six years old, before she had ever seen a

Holocaust movie. In the dream she was in a packed room, standing next to her mother.

> I was a young child, so I didn't understand what was going on. There was heightened emotion around me. First, I was just standing next to my mother. I felt her strength, her love. I trusted her. Then I held onto her leg, which was eye-level for me. It became hard to breathe. I would wake up gasping for air.
>
> I remember not wanting to have this dream again because of waking up not being able to breathe. The dreams were not scary while they were happening. But it was scary when I woke up and couldn't breathe.

Doris Ellen Applebaum was born in Passaic, New Jersey, in 1944 to a Jewish family. For many years during her childhood she had a recurring dream.

> I dreamt of walking with a group of people through a dark, dimly lit tunnel. I heard mocking voices on both sides. There was a big door that I was approaching. I heard a mocking voice laughing with derision, and the voice said derisively, "And now do you believe your God exists?"
>
> I answered, "Yes." And the dream would end before the door was opened.

Nechama Bornstein, a Jewish woman from Denmark, born in 1963, had a dream as an adult:

In the dream, I was walking with a group of people through a darkened passage. At the end of this hallway, there was a wall made of brown wooden planks. The ceiling was low. The wall to the left was set with white-painted bricks.... I knew that we were being taken to be punished. We had done something terrible, according to the Nazis. We were herded on, close together.... Then, right before the end of the hallway, on the right, a door was slightly open. We were pushed through it and entered a fairly large room. It was lit, but I didn't see any source of light....

Years later, a traveling exhibition of children's photos from Auschwitz was held in The Architect Academy in Copenhagen.

A small photograph on the wall caught my attention.... [It] wasn't showing a face, but a low-ceiling hallway. My heart started pounding. I moved forward, every step seemed to take an eternity, unfolding in another time dimension. I knew this place. There it was—the wall made of wooden planks, then that of white-painted bricks.... I was so upset, I could hardly breathe. I reached the small photograph. This was where we had been walking [in the dream]. There was the door to the right.

A small sign beneath the photograph read: "Entrance to the gas chamber at Auschwitz."[26]

---

26. From Nechama Bornstein's unpublished memoir, "*The Photograph*."

CHAPTER 4

PUTTING THE DREAM PIECES TOGETHER

WHILE THE DREAMS CITED in the previous chapter have been of single (traumatic) scenes, some people sent me emails of what I call "narrative dreams." These dreamers see themselves in many different episodes of the same lifetime, which they piece together as a coherent narrative.

For example, Carmen Stark, who was born into a Methodist family in Bellingham, Washington, in 1965, had many dreams of a Jewish woman named Esther, who had five children and lived in Germany.

> The first time I started dreaming of her (that I can remember) I was four or so. I had a lot of dreams that made kind of a story once I pieced them together. Unfortunately, the most recurrent dream

was of her death. I haven't had these dreams for years now, but the memories of them are seared into my brain. I can picture her house, her kitchen, her children. I know what dress she wore when she died.

Growing up, Carmen was completely obsessed with the Holocaust. "Every other kid was doing reports on the life stages of a frog, and mine were about Dachau, Bergen-Belsen, and Kristallnacht. I read everything about the Holocaust and wrote essays about it all through grade school. My parents thought there was something wrong with me, so I eventually stopped."

Georgene Powell was born in 1946 in Phoenix, Arizona, to a Christian family that never once mentioned the Holocaust. Strangely, the first story she ever wrote, when she was in fifth grade, was about the Holocaust.

In her thirties and forties, Georgene started to have dreams:

The following are the dreams as I remember them:
I can see the house where I lived in what I believe to be Frankfurt. It was a tall row house, dark brown in color with a front stoop and three steps leading down to the street. The inside was a wide staircase and dark walls, perhaps an upper middle-class home. I felt terror standing at the bottom of the steps, knowing that I would find my mother dead. I knew instinctively that she had hung herself rather than hold us back as we prepared to leave the country. My dream did not show me going up the

stairs to find her. I couldn't make myself climb the stairs. I was too horrified, and the dream ended.

In another dream, a woman is with a group of people, surrounded by soldiers. She is hauled into the middle. She's wearing a knee-length coat. The captain hits her, and another captive screams, "No!" He's hit with the butt end of a rifle by another soldier and is knocked out. I feel that the woman is me, and I am terrified. The man is my husband. I screamed when he fell to the ground, as he did when I was yanked from his side. Was he killed then? I don't know. I can still see his face.

The dream about my death was also very vivid but longer. I died in the camp and left my body. It was like there was a fog (no bright light). I moved towards a group of people, and a man said, "Welcome back, Doctor." In my waking state, I had no idea that I was a doctor. I was always under the impression that my husband was a doctor. Could a woman have been a doctor back then? Probably. I found that a bit puzzling, but it could be true.

Anyway, in the dream, I nodded at the people who welcomed me back to the "other world" and went in search of my daughter, finding her in a strange building, not the family home, as she was about to jump from the window. She had been trying to pass as a gentile but had been outed and decided that suicide was better than being taken. I tell her not to jump. She will die. But the girl does jump, dies, and immediately finds me, her mother. She tells me that she is free, and it feels so good.

Psychoanalysts have long recommended writing down one's dreams immediately upon awakening in order to cultivate the ability to remember them. Rachel B., born to a Christian family in Montana in 1972, has an MA in psychology. For years she meticulously recorded her dreams on her computer immediately upon awakening. At one point, she printed out scores of pages of her Holocaust-related dreams and shared them with her husband. He was so horrified and disapproving that an embarrassed Rachel shredded the papers.

A few years later, after she began corresponding with me about her childhood dreams and phobias of Germans, she located the files of her dreams still in her computer. She pieced together the snippets of her dreams into chronological order so that it reads like one narrative.

I started having dreams when I was in elementary school. The only thing I remember from them is being chased and fleeing for my very life. People were screaming in German, and, though I had never met anyone from Germany, I knew it was German I was hearing.

From a very young age, I would tell my parents I was terrified of Germans and that they are murderers. My parents had no context in which to understand it because we knew no Germans and did not live in a part of the country with a large Germanic population. My father's people are Scottish and Irish, and I was surrounded by that cultural context....

I first found out about the Holocaust in junior high.

In the first [adult] dream, I was talking to my elderly Jewish grandmother, and we were being separated. Her last words to me were that I cannot forget "Havdalah." Everything came down to remembering "Havdalah." And then we were separated. I was taken one way, and she was taken another. I had never heard this word, and when I woke up I had to look up what it meant. It is a formal service that ends the Jewish Sabbath.

I had dreams of being in a wealthy Viennese family—one that was proudly assimilated, but still practicing Jewish traditions. We lived in a beautiful home—a large apartment in the city with a back garden. We felt much pride in the fact that we were doctors and scientists and had become successful in the Austrian culture. We considered ourselves Austrians first and trusted those around us. Our house had grandfather clocks, oriental rugs, and beautiful wood furniture. I wore beautifully made custom dresses, and our father made sure me, my sisters, and my mom never wanted for anything. I wanted to be a scientist or a doctor.

My name was Sophie. I saw myself in the mirror. I had an enormous head of curly, long black hair, porcelain skin, and large green eyes. I wore beautiful, tailored suits that accentuated my slim waist. I took pride in being able to pass as a Viennese girl. Basically, I was spoiled and imma-ture and was prouder to be Viennese than Jewish. I believed I was one of them and that we could all get along. I believed pogroms were a thing of the past and that the non-Jewish Viennese were forward thinking, and I believed they accepted us. I reasoned these were cultured people and that there should be no distinction between Jews and non-Jews.

In another dream, I remember the deep betray-al I felt when we realized that the Austrians would never truly see us as one of them. I felt the fear of being hunted—almost as if I were a wild animal. No one saw my humanity any longer. They saw me as something other than human, less than human. I remember not knowing who to trust, and that was painful.

In another dream, I was separated from my family and very confused. I remember the inde-scribable pain—like nothing on earth—and pow-erlessness of being separated from my family.

In another dream, I was grabbed by my hair, thrown on the ground, and had a gun put to my head for sport. They did not kill me. They just laughed and thought it was fun to inspire fear and the idea that I no longer owned myself—I was at their will. And it was a lesson to the others around me—they too had no autonomy, and our lives

were determined by their will over us. I remember
the extreme sense of betrayal, the inability to understand why or how this could happen. It felt like
it was the end of the world.

While the dreams cited above came in bits and pieces, one
woman anonymously sent me a single dream she had as an
adult. It is so long and detailed that I was tempted to dismiss
it as fiction. The writer identified herself only as a Chareidi,
American-born Jewish woman now living in Israel. In the
dream she is a non-Jewish woman living a life of debauchery
in a European country.

I include it here for two reasons. First, the woman herself
is so embarrassed by the dream, not only because of her immoral way of life but also because she was cold-hearted and
dispassionate, a complete repudiation of the values she cher-
ishes in this lifetime. Secondly, she herself is ambivalent about
identifying it as a past-life dream. As she wrote to me:

Now I guess you understand why I am being completely anonymous. I feel that this is some kind of
past-life reflection. But what if it was just a dream?
If so, I seem really not normal…. And it's embar-
rassing, not only because of the "profession,"
but also because of what a cold, unsentimental,
empty, numb person I was. No heart, no soul. Just
completely focused on myself and making money;
basically, just getting through the day. And you
can't even say I was heroic. I felt I was taking no
risk….

I feel horribly exposed in writing this to you, and I have no proof that this wasn't just a dream, but at the same time, I feel compelled to share this with you.

I dreamed I was this hard, cold woman, maybe in my late forties, running a thriving immoral establishment. Anyway, a woman brought me several silent, sad children through the back door to the kitchen and pleaded with me to hide them. She kept reassuring me that the children knew how to keep perfectly silent and be perfectly still.

I was going to say no, but then she said, "They'll be killed if you don't take them in." I looked at them, and they looked so small and sad—and perfectly silent—and their sheer stillness made my decision. (It sounds horrible, but if the children had shown any emotion, or smiled, or tried to engage me, I would have turned them away.) I gestured to the cellar door in the floor and said, "Put them down there." The woman said her goodbyes to the children, reminding them to remain perfectly silent. They didn't cry or smile; they seemed resigned. Then she watched as they went down the steps, and she left.

I have a vague feeling that my maid/cook was there and that she went along with me (shocked at my benevolence). Also, I felt no fear whatsoever. I was numb from living the kind of life I'd been living for so long, and anyway was one hundred percent certain that no search of Jewish children would occur (who would ever suspect such a place of hiding

Jewish children?). I was doing black market stuff, too, so I felt like I was providing so many necessary services that no one was going to mess with me—and that I could also bribe or blackmail anyone who tried.

I don't know how long I hid them in the cellar. Maybe a year or less. During that time, I instructed the cook to feed them generously. I would also lift open the cellar door periodically to ask the children if they needed anything. Whenever we got a shipment of smuggled goods like chocolate and other goodies (fruits?), I'd lift open the cellar door, toss down the goodies to the children, and drop it shut. (Completely unsentimental.) So the children were living in a dark, airless cellar, but they were very well-fed with a variety of high-quality foods. That was important to me, but not in any sentimental way.

One of the times, I asked them what they wanted. One of the older girls said softly, "My brother isn't well. He needs some air. Can he come out, even for just a little while? We won't make any noise." I lifted the door higher to get a better look at them and thought, *Yeah, he really doesn't look too good. In fact, none of them do.* And then, *Children need to run about.*

I told them to come out, and then I took them out up a path that led to a small building that housed a dance hall, in some woods. It was dusty, having been unused for a while, and chairs were stacked all about, and round tables stood against the walls.

A large window looked out toward the path. I remember thinking that I had better stay with them because I felt it wasn't safe for their sakes to leave them there unsupervised, that someone could hurt them. So I leaned against the opposite wall so that I could see if anyone would be coming, and the children just stood around, maybe stumbled a bit.

After that, I took them there every day for hours. At first, they were timid and just stood there or walked about. Eventually, they started running back and forth, back and forth. They even started playing among the stacks of chairs and under the tables. They never made a sound with their mouths, but their eyes were totally lit up as they raced back and forth from end to end, again and again, and there was a hint of a smile around their mouths.

I would stand there the whole time, smoking with a cigarette holder and thinking and feeling nothing, just completely blank and sort of sour. I'm not sure, but the atmosphere was as if either the war was over or winding down and felt like it was over in my little part of the village. There was no business of any type at that point, so I had time to just loiter there with the children.

At one point, I noticed that their clothes were shabby, and I told my maid to go buy the best-quality children's clothes, whatever the price. But again, this was done with a complete lack of feeling.

So there I was waiting for I don't know what, and then I see a dark figure come to the main house and knock on the door. Moments later, he is coming up the path while looking back and gesturing thanks (the maid gave him directions). I frown, and the children immediately freeze. I don't recognize the man, but I can tell by his gait that he is a cheerful, energetic sort, and as he comes closer, I see he is a Jew. (Long black jacket and pants, brown beard, a hat, round glasses, and hawkish nose.) He gives me a big smile (I think he doesn't know what I do). I give him a hard look. He explains that he is gathering Jewish orphans, and he heard that there were some hidden here. I relax a tad and gesture behind him.

He turns around and is thrilled to see them, and then he does a double take. "Why—they look—they look wonderful!" He can't get over their clothes and their healthy weight. He's so excited that he stammers and stutters as he talks. The children, recognizing him as a rabbi, eagerly surround him with glowing faces. He talks to them and asks them questions, and they happily and softly answer. I don't understand what they're saying. (Indicating that he is speaking to them in another language? Perhaps Yiddish?)

He turns to me, practically speechless with joy and amazement. He tells me that the children told him how I always fed them, even gave them special foods like chocolate, and how I bought them clothes and how I take them every day to this hall for hours so they can run and play.

It doesn't really compute that the children are grateful to me and even like me. I'm apathetic throughout all his gushing. "I have recovered many children!" he enthuses, "and I have never seen children so well taken care of! They look absolutely wonderful!"

I do not even bother looking at him. I'm holding my cigarette holder and staring in another direction, waiting for them to all just go away, but he says, "I must repay you."

That catches my attention and I look back at him, but realize that this guy has no real money. Yeah, I'll take whatever he gives, no matter the pittance, because that's the kind of person I am, but it won't be anything to get excited about. I've got enough money anyhow, from all the illegal activities. I don't need his money. I see by the look on his face that he's trying to think of how to repay me—which means that he really doesn't have any money at all.

With a smile, he declares, "I bless you that in your next life, you'll be a Jew!"

Shocked, my head whips around to give him a venomous look. "What?!" I hiss. I am deeply insulted and outraged. The bizarreness of being reincarnated doesn't occur to me. I am seething that he blesses me to be a Jew. It's almost like he's making fun of me in a really sick way.

But he doesn't even look at me. He is nodding to himself with pleasure and satisfaction and says, "Yes, yes, that's right" and repeats the blessing. I am still glaring at him. He notices and chuckles, telling me, "Don't worry; you'll like it!"

Then he and the children go, and I just feel relief combined with a kind of dark emptiness. My life is totally empty and meaningless.

Then I woke up.

She ended her account, "In case you're wondering...the rabbi was right. I do really like being Jewish."[27]

---

27. The dream, as fascinating as it is, poses a theological problem in Judaism. According to Kabbalah, a Jewish soul is a specific kind of soul. Jewish souls can incarnate as Jews, meaning they are born to a Jewish mother, or can incarnate as non-Jews for various reasons (which is discussed in detail in chapter 8, "Jewish Souls in Christian Bodies"). In addition, a person can acquire a Jewish soul through conversion according to *halachah*, but not through a rabbi giving a blessing. So how could this madam, who was clearly not a Jewish soul, be born as a Jew in this lifetime?

I wrote back, asking for more details of her life. Her response solved the theological conundrum. Her father was Jewish, but not her mother. She was, however, raised Jewish, and only as a young adult realized that she had to undergo a halachic conversion, which she did. "I grew up sure I was one hundred percent Jewish, and was very traumatized to discover that I was not. I've hardly told anyone of my true status because I have shame about it, which I discovered is very common among people who grew up thinking they were Jewish but actually weren't. I wouldn't even be telling you if I wasn't totally anonymous."

So this is how the rabbi's blessing was actualized. In this lifetime, she underwent a conversion and became a Jew.

CHAPTER 5

INNER QUICKSAND: FLASHBACKS AND PANIC ATTACKS

MELANIE, GROWING UP IN A CHRISTIAN FAMILY in Scarborough, Ontario, Canada, in the 1960s, had what she called, "a happy childhood until about four or five years old, when my memory came back." As she describes the traumatic experience:

> When I was four or five, my mother took me to school to register me for kindergarten. As we approached the school on foot and I saw the chain-link fence and paved yard, I began to feel very nervous. I began to ask my mother repeatedly where the train was. She kept replying that there was no train, that we were at a school (there was no train station near our home).

We entered the yard, and very quickly the scene "switched" and I saw a brick building (this is how I remember it). I then saw long lines of people in front of wooden desks with people behind them with clipboards and lists. I insisted I didn't want to go, and again, where was the train? It must be on the other side of the building. I asked my mom if she was coming with me, to which she replied, "No, you go to school on your own."

I began to cry and to try to get away from my mother. I knew the train led to death. I knew I had been about the same age in my last life when I took the train alone. I knew I had been in hiding with about four or five random adults. They often whispered together. One day I made a sound. They whispered and decided to give me up so I would not jeopardize the group. A woman from the group, or maybe she was the one hiding us, took me to the train. (*I hated her* for taking me to the train station.) She was stoic and curt, dispassionate. She took me to the desk with the woman who had the clipboard and a list.

Next thing I remember is being the small child in a boxcar at a level where I could smell the human waste, at a level that I could not escape. I remember I had dark, dark hair and eyes. (It seems cruel to be blond haired and blue eyed in this life and be fussed over for my looks by German neighbors!)

Anyway, I was making such a fuss in the school-yard that another mother came over to my mom.

"I've heard of this," she told my mom. "This child has lived before."

My mom scoffed and said, "No! She got this from TV." The other mother said my reaction was too severe to be from TV and must be real. I was sitting on the ground refusing to budge, so the other mother knelt down and asked me what I remembered. Then she touched my back, and at this I was back in the schoolyard, speechless.

My own mother did not believe me (so this is not a story I share, and even my two brothers do not know it). I kept quiet, and my mom said, "See, she just got it from TV." But I hadn't.

A flashback is a sudden, disturbing, and vivid memory of an event in the past, typically as the result of psychological trauma. Flashbacks are common in people who suffer from post-traumatic stress disorder (PTSD). Unlike normal memories, in a flashback the person reexperiences the traumatic event as if in the present. According to psychologist Tom Bunn, "[The] experience is not of remembering an event, but of living the event. In an explicit flashback, the person is involuntarily transported back in time. To the person, it does not seem so. What they experience is being experienced as if it were happening in the present."[28]

Flashbacks of past lives are also the sudden reliving of a traumatic scene, but in this case the time period and location

---

28. Tom Bunn, "Is What You Are Feeling a Flashback?" *Psychology Today*, August 15, 2014, https://www.psychologytoday.com/us/blog/conquer-fear-flying/201408/is-what-you-are-feeling-flashback.

are unrelated to the person's experiences in this lifetime. Mary is a devout church-going Protestant who lives in Alabama and is keenly aware that her Church considers reincarnation a doctrine of the Devil. She therefore had no way to understand what happened to her one day in 1987 when she went to pick up her son from band practice. The school had recently hired a young Jewish man as band director.

> The woman who was president of the parents' association had said some things I felt were prejudiced. When I went to pick up my child from band practice that day, I went with the intention of meeting this man and forming my own opinion. When I arrived, several parents were in a very abusive conversation with him over his new rules for the students.
>
> One minute I was standing in the schoolyard, and the next I was in a courtyard of a building built with gray stones. The roofs were made of tile. The weather was cloudy and cold and looked like it would soon snow. When I looked around me, I saw men, women, and children. The women wore long coats, and scarves over their heads tied in a manner that completely covered their hair. The men wore long coats and caps and had long beards. The little boys wore short pants with jackets, caps, and long socks that covered their legs. All of these people's clothing were of drab colors and looked worn. The other people in the courtyard were soldiers in dark brown with rifles in their arms.

> A small boy said to me, "Why do they hate us
> so?" I remember thinking, *They are the Nazis, we
> are the Jews, and they are going to kill us.*
> Then I was back in the schoolyard. I believe the
> band director was the little boy who spoke to me.

Flashbacks are typically triggered by a situation or setting similar to the previous traumatic experience. My terror in Vienna at the age of twenty-one, described in the prologue, was a flashback.

Ironically, I had adamantly refused to go to Germany, but amicably agreed to go to Austria, which I associated with Strauss waltzes and pastries, naively unaware that it had been the birthplace of Hitler and a hotbed of Nazism. The residential neighborhood whose buildings were unchanged from the World War II period, and specifically the corners of the streets, triggered the trauma of being chased by Aryan ruffians. I heard their catcalls and felt them behind me. I ran, sweating and terrified, not because I remembered a past danger, but because I felt gripped by a present danger. In a flashback, the present does not recall the past but is replaced by it.

On New Year's Eve of 1969, a hippie named Claudia Antell went to a giant rock concert in Los Angeles "to celebrate the dawning of the New Age."

> There were many acts, and there were light shows
> throbbing on the walls. Some people were staring
> in worshipful, awestruck wonder at the light shows,
> most were just enjoying the music. There were no
> seats, not really a theater, just a huge, open hall.

At midnight, the main act came on—Canned Heat (also played at Woodstock). "Bear," the leader of the band, a huge hairy guy with a big bushy beard, came out, dressed as Baby New Year, riding atop an elephant. Quite the spectacle. Coming from the back corner of the hall, he had to cross the hall diagonally to get to the stage. The crowd parted to make way for the elephant. Bear, way up high, was holding his hand aloft with two fingers parted, in the peace symbol. The crowd responded. All hands raised. Peace.

Then he passed me, and the crowd closed in behind him, all pressing forward, only it wasn't a bunch of hippies making peace symbols anymore. They were all Nazis going "*Heil Hitler*"! I hid my face in terror. Every time I peeked through my fingers, I saw the same frightening scene.

Years later, living in Philly, I was out walking one day near the Parkway. A marching band came by. Kids, really. Teenage boys in black uniforms trimmed in red, playing drums and other instruments. And again, Nazis! Instant, complete terror caused me to bolt and run and run and run in mortal fear, crying, till I couldn't run anymore. At the same time that I can tell you that I know these weren't really Nazis, and that there was no "real" reason to be terrified, I wasn't confused about why I was running. There was a part of me that understood the terror of mortal fear of Nazis so thoroughly that there was no question about why I felt terrified and why I ran.

The only question was, *Where did that come from?*
It came from the same place as the New Year's Eve
experience.

People who experience flashbacks of the Holocaust usually have had Holocaust-related dreams and often phobias. For example, a woman born in Cape Town, South Africa, in 1976 and adopted at birth by a Christian family started dreaming of the death camps at the age of nine, although no one had ever told her about the Holocaust. She has a phobia of the German language. "Whenever I hear German, I want to cover my ears and run away. I get panicky and sweaty, and I need to leave, be it in a room or even in an elevator."

Her flashbacks are specific and horrifying: "I experience having my husband and kids killed, then being tortured and left starving before hanging myself in a dark room during the snow with the sounds of and what looks like SS officers outside." She describes herself as "completely obsessed" with the Holocaust. "I am completely drawn to the suffering and cannot control my fear, shaking, and immense feeling of being back there."

Many people describe their flashbacks as "visions" for which they have no logical explanation. A woman who is an executive in a high-tech company in Silicon Valley was born to a Jewish family in San Diego in 1966.

Since I was eight years old, I've had visions of being in the showers being gassed with many other women and children. Even when I would get into my own shower, I would sometimes feel dread, but I did not understand why. In these visions I saw myself as a child. They always started and ended in the room of the gas chamber. As an adult, I still see the vision, but less often.

I do have visions at times when I see trains; I see trains rushing by with Jews trapped inside, en route to a concentration camp. Yesterday, for example, a train passed by with a loud shrill, and I imagined Jews sitting on that train on their way to a concentration camp—a very random thought on a beautiful sunny day in California.

Joan, a radio and TV personality born to a Jewish family in Pennsylvania in 1946, also reported a "vision."

In 2003, I was gardening when my vision "changed," and I found myself in a crowded room with many other people. We were standing and waiting for something. I was holding an infant, rocking him and crooning into his ear a lovely soft tune that seemed to soothe him. I knew this was not my child, and that his mother was no longer able to hold him.

The force of this vision brought me to my knees on the bare ground, and a massive feeling of sorrow and loss overcame me. The song I hummed was unknown to me. Still under the effects of this vision, I managed to stumble into the house and reach the piano, because I needed to preserve this tune. But by the time I reached the living room, I imagine because of the physical effort that may have overwhelmed whatever mental process was taking place, the tune vanished.

It was a whole year before I heard, while listening to TV music from another room, The Tune. I ran in to see its title on the screen, but it was just turning off as I got into the room. However, I saw enough to see that it was a lullaby, and it was Eastern European.

I have had no doubt that this vision was of me as a very young woman holding and soothing perhaps a sibling in a gas chamber as we waited for the end. My imagination tells me that I had been taken to die with my mother, who might have been so distraught that she could no longer think of anyone else. So I held my baby brother. But this part was not included in the vision.

While Joan's flashback seems to have occurred spontaneously, usually flashbacks are triggered by a place or situation reminiscent of the trauma. Judith Shakury was born to a Jewish family in Budapest, Hungary. When she was twelve years old, she was walking along the Danube in Budapest when she suddenly experienced herself as a woman being shot in the back and falling into the river.

I know the exact spot where I fell into the Danube. I know the feeling, that it was a relief, the cold water and the end of running, and those soldiers and dogs behind me.

Twelve-year-old Judith continued her walk, but when she returned and passed the same spot, she had the same flashback.

Living now in the United States, Judith read about the Shoes on the Danube Bank memorial erected in 2005, in memory of the victims shot into the Danube by Arrow Cross militiamen in 1944 to 1945. "I wonder if it's even in the right area," wonders Judith, whose flashback is to her an actual historic fact. "It was more towards the Szent István Park *rakpart*, before Margit Bridge."

Sandra was born in New Jersey in 1950 and adopted by Protestant parents. Growing up, the Holocaust was never mentioned in her home. Yet, inexplicably, the sight of a streetlight on snow triggered a nightly flashback.

> When I was about seven years old, I knew I'd had another "life." Put to bed in my room, I'd look out the window at the snow and the streetlight across the street and recall when I had been a young Jewish boy named Josef in a Polish ghetto. Crouching in the dark, in a corner of my room (as on a street corner), I could feel the damp, cold, hunger, and loneliness. Everything was gray and dismal. I spent many hours like this.
>
> The first time I saw *Schindler's List*, I "recognized" the rooms, buildings, and streets of the Kraków Ghetto. Although I feel I recalled life in the ghetto, I am not certain what became of me; nor do I have any recollections of transports, concentration camps, or being sent to a gas chamber.

Sometimes a flashback can be triggered by a sound. A man born to a Jewish family in Brooklyn in 1970 had both

Holocaust-related dreams that have pursued him from child-hood until the present, and a dramatic flashback at the age of eighteen.

I was in an auto repair shop with a friend of mine. The sound of the impact wrench removing a wheel from a car triggered off a memory of my death. I was very puzzled for years from this memory, and didn't understand it.

In the memory, I was standing around a very large pit with a group of people. Some military men were standing with machine guns in the back-ground. I tried not to look around, and felt very exhausted, but I knew that my life was about to end. I saw very tall trees in the forest with leaves on the top. These trees weren't like any that I've seen growing up in America. The temperature was pleasant, with good weather. It looked like the summertime.

Suddenly, one officer said three words in a foreign language that I wasn't able to understand. I would assume that he said, "Ready, aim, fire." The officers holding machine guns started to fire in sequence from the far-right hand corner of the pit, then continued along the pit to the left. I was somewhere in the middle or the far left. People being shot in the back of the head were falling forward into the pit, and I knew that it would be my turn in a matter of seconds. As soon as he got up to me, I felt very light-headed, with a dizzy feeling, then started to fall forward headfirst into the pit just like everybody else. When I was falling forward, everything started to get dark, until it was completely dark.

At this point I came out of my flashback, and my friend was next to me. He was looking at me the whole time, and tried to talk to me, but I didn't respond. He asked me what was wrong, and I said that I didn't know, and couldn't explain it. After trying to analyze it, I told him about it.

Part two of this event occurred when I was thirty-six (eighteen years later). I was in a shul. The rabbi was giving some sort of speech, and he might have mentioned something about the Holocaust, which trigged another flashback. This time I was more tuned into the flashback, since it had happened before. I was in a wooden boxcar that was like a section of a train. It was made out of wooden strips. A little light was able to come through some of the strips. I was on top of a pile of bodies, and didn't know who was alive or dead. The stench was unbearable, and my heart was pounding so hard it felt like it was going to come out of my chest.

I didn't know where I was going to be taken or why I was in this boxcar. Everything was quiet except for the double tapping noise of the wheels hitting the tracks. It sounded almost like a heartbeat. One pounding sound with another sound immediately after it, then a brief pause with another double pounding sound of the front and rear wheels going over the tracks.

It took a little time to figure out, but it seems like this event occurred first. I had to be put into this boxcar before I was brought to the large pit to be shot. I don't know why I had these memories in reverse order in eighteen-year intervals.

I was always private about these things and didn't discuss them with counselors. I told a few close friends and my wife about these memories, but never discussed them with my son or my parents. Until reading your article [on Aish.com], I didn't know that so many people have past memories like mine.

Because a flashback is a reliving of an event, it is often accompanied by smells or feelings of heat or cold. A woman born to a Catholic family in Chicago in 1963 has horrific memories that she terms "a waking flashback":

I remember just white tiles, being bare, freezing, sick. I was a young man. (I'm a woman in this life.) There were many others in the same room with me, and then all went black.

Yes, I was definitely gassed with many others in the room. We were shoulder to shoulder, crammed into a cold room. I had trouble standing, it was freezing. I was weak and sick. That is really all I can remember or recall. This was a "reality," a "waking flashback" is the perfect description, not a dream. Frequently I see this. The tiles were white and I was shoved facing them, and whenever I see white tiles in this life, I have instant terrifying flashbacks.

All I know is that I was terrified and so cold in that room. I could barely walk, and my clothing had been taken from me. It was humiliating. I kept my head down. I don't remember sounds, just being shoved in that room. I saw the tiles, and then black.

Sometimes the trigger of a flashback is not a sensory stimulation, such as a sound or sight, but rather an emotion. For Doris Ellen Applebaum, born in 1947 to a Jewish family in Passaic, New Jersey, the feeling of being the butt of anti-Semitism elicited a flashback. In October 1978, she had "a hostile job interview" in New York City.

A man who may have been Arab was one of the interviewers, and he expressed significant hostility toward me. That's what set it off. Walking down Times Square, I suddenly had a flashback. It was dusty and near a train. I was about fourteen years old. My mother was told to get into a different line than I was, and she made a lunge toward me. A German officer ordered a young soldier to shoot my mother. He did, and the terror was stuck in my throat. In 1978—in reliving this—I let out a scream that had been buried inside of me, and I began to cry.

The person experiencing the flashback knows clearly that he or she is undergoing a process dramatically different than simple memory. While memory takes place inside a person's mind, a flashback pulls the person inside the memory. For example, Samantha, born in Boulder, Colorado, in 1985 to a Jewish mother and a Christian father, had one flashback:

> At age nine I went into an altered state one night and saw myself as a child in a crowded European train station. It was packed with displaced people in 1940s clothing. People had many suitcases, and were wearing many layers of clothing. Families were waiting to be put on the trains. I had gotten lost and was going around asking people if they had seen my parents.

The fascinating case of Carmen Maria Rodriguez combines a flashback, panic attacks, déjà vu, and Holocaust obsession with a bizarre biographical rerun. Carmen Maria was born in Havana, Cuba, in 1955 to a Catholic family.

> At the age of five, in the midst of one of the Communist demonstrations against my family be-cause we were wealthy, I looked out from the porch in terror at the masses yelling at us, and looked down to the ground and had this thought: *Oh no, no, no, it cannot be happening again!!!* While look-ing down at the floor, I saw banners, really red, with a black sign on them. Later on, I recognized these signs as swastikas.

Throughout her life, Carmen Maria, who converted to Judaism at the age of forty-seven, had an extreme emotional reaction to anything connected to the Holocaust. In college in New York, when taking courses in Jewish literature, she had to ask the professor to exempt her from reading Holocaust literature.

> I could not stand, endure, tolerate, or survive read-
> ing Holocaust literature. I would be in a NYC subway,
> bawling my eyes out. The professor realized how
> much it affected me, and I was not required to read
> further.
> When working in Austria during the 1993 UN
> International Conference of Human Rights, I re-
> fused, utterly refused, to participate in any of the
> trips or outings to extermination camps. It was too
> much for me to bear, and I would lose my breath
> just thinking of traveling there. I made up all sorts
> of excuses.

It is interesting that Carmen Maria's one flashback was of a raging mob, reminiscent of the earliest stage of Nazi anti-Semitism, but, unlike virtually all the others who re-ported flashbacks, she had no dreams of fleeing, ghettos, gas chambers, or death pits. Her panicky reactions as an adult are to the Holocaust in general, devoid of the specific horrors recounted by others. It is almost as if in her former life, although traumatized, she escaped the Holocaust some-time between the riots of Kristallnacht, which took place in November 1938, and the Nazis' violent persecution and killing of Jews, which began with the German invasion of Poland in September 1939.

Carmen Maria solved this mystery for herself while on a professional trip to Germany. At the age of six, she had been sent out of Cuba alone to the United States on Operation Peter Pan, a campaign to save over fourteen thousand unaccompanied Cuban children from the clutches of Fidel Castro. Strangely, as an adult Carmen Maria was in Berlin at a train station when she was overcome by a feeling of intense sadness. Later she discovered that that very train platform was the place of departure of the Kindertransports, an operation to save unaccompanied Jewish children from the clutches of Hitler by sending them to Great Britain.

Was she in a former incarnation one of the children of the Kindertransports, which began in December 1938, and, although it saved the children's lives, left most of them with severe trauma? Reflecting on this, Carmen Maria comments, "There was a repeat in my life of what was before."

Unlike flashbacks, panic attacks are not the actual reliving of a past experience. Rather, panic attacks are an intense emotional and physical reaction: a rapid, pounding heart rate; sweating; trembling or shaking; feeling dizzy or faint; shortness of breath; feelings of heat or cold; and/or a sense of impending doom or danger. A panic attack is to a normal emotional reaction what a bomb is to a firecracker. For example, when visiting a Holocaust museum feeling sadness, horror, and anger is normal; fainting, crying hysterically, and inability to breathe is a panic attack.

Bonnie Reiss, born to a Jewish family in Brooklyn, New York, in 1958, was a child when she viewed a documentary about the Holocaust. "I broke down hysterically. I rarely read anything connected to the Holocaust because I get panicky. At my first visit to the Holocaust Museum in Washington, DC, while looking at a model of a crematoria, I couldn't breathe."

Sharon Gordon was born to a Jewish family in London in 1964. Twice when she visited Yad Vashem, the iconic World Holocaust Remembrance Center in Jerusalem, she experienced panic attacks.

Rhonnie Goldfader was born to a Jewish family in St. Louis, Missouri, in 1951. She wrote:

> I remember when I was about five or six, my parents would take us to the local movie theater, where they would usually have a double feature on Sundays. Afterwards, we'd go to my grandmother's for dinner. One Sunday, my mom said we couldn't stay for both movies, as we had to get to my grandmother's early. I was this little snotty kid and made a stink, saying, "I want to see both movies."
>
> After the first one was over, my mom said that we could stay and see some of the second movie. I remember that movie starting as if it were yesterday. On the screen (this movie was in black and white), there appeared a huge Nazi flag, a Nazi officer, and a bunch of kids. I remember it was raining in the film. After about two minutes, I remember pounding on the seat, crying, and screaming, "Let's get out of here. Let's leave now!" I got off my seat and climbed under the seat in front of me to escape having to see the screen. I remember my mom saying to me,

"What is wrong with you? You just begged me to see both movies and now you want to leave?" We did leave the theater.

I cannot listen to, read, or see a movie about the Holocaust without crying and possibly having a panic attack. I would never, ever go to a Holocaust museum; I can never, I mean *ever*, see anything Holocaust related. When in Israel, I would never go to Yad Vashem or any other Holocaust museum. I never saw *Schindler's List* or other movies of similar topics; I can't even hear someone talk about it. I start to cry and get physically sick. I am on the verge of a panic attack whenever the Holocaust is discussed; I remove myself from the conversation.

A man born to a Catholic family in Newport Beach, California, in 1957 was "secretly obsessed with the 1920s and 30s; my fascination has always stopped abruptly at 1940." One day at the age of twenty-two, he was browsing in a bookstore and came across a picture book about the Holocaust.

I became absolutely frozen with fear and froze for about an hour, pretty much unable to move. My breathing felt heavy and labored. I was finally able to leave the store only by taking the heaviest and stiffest jerky steps with Herculean effort. I was so embarrassed at all this, although no one else seemed to notice. As I drove home, I felt my head spinning.

> After that I was haunted about the Holocaust with daily obsessive intrusive thoughts for about the next decade. Reading Corrie Ten Boom's *The Hiding Place* relieved it temporarily. But after a while the terrifying obsession came back again. The thing that finally gave me reasonable relief was reading *Hasidic Tales of the Holocaust* [by Yaffa Eliach]. I used to wish I could go to support groups for children of Holocaust survivors, but I never did, for obvious reasons.

As an educator, he tried to find a scientific explanation for his panic attack in the bookstore and his obsessive daydreams. He concluded that, although his father was Catholic and his mother Protestant, perhaps he had Jewish ancestry, and epigenetics would explain what otherwise had no rational explanation. He recently did a DNA test with Ancestry.com, and found that he has less than 1 percent Jewish ancestry.

"So how do I account for my experiences?" he reflects. "In some ways I still feel as though I could be a Holocaust survivor with haunted memories, as someone who has done their best to move on. Yet I believe it only fair to emphasize that I could never feel this on a scale of a true survivor, of course." He is left with the mystery. NORE.

A woman born to a Christian family in the United States had horrifying dreams as a young child. At the age of twelve, she came across a book about the Holocaust. "I wanted to throw up," she recalls, "because it was so similar to the dreams I had had as a kid." She felt so strongly drawn to Judaism that, at the age of twenty, she converted.

Years later, she read a true Holocaust story about a four-year-old Jewish girl in Poland who was being herded into a boxcar with her mother. Suddenly, the mother shoved her daughter off the train and told her to "run to the park and play with the goyim." The child was adopted by a Polish family, and twelve years later married their son. Reading this story, "it felt like déjà vu, and I literally had a panic attack. I have a very strong feeling that I am connected to that mother's soul."

Just as books about the Holocaust can set off a panic attack, some souls are triggered by Holocaust movies or TV shows. One woman born to a Catholic family in London in 1953 was watching *The World at War* on television at the age of fourteen with her father. "They showed footage of Auschwitz. I was horrified to recognize a corridor leading to a gas chamber. I went into a panic attack—sobbing uncontrollably, shaking, and screaming to my father. I knew where it was. I described it to my father as the camera was following the presenter through the corridor."

Sandra L. Johnson was born in Chicago to Catholic parents from Finland. As a child she had recurring dreams of men coming into her house and attacking and beating her father. She would wake up and tell her mother about the dream. Her mother would dismiss it, assuring her that her father was at work and was just fine. Holocaust movies trigger panic attacks in Sandra.

Chaya Goldstein was born to a Jewish family in Brooklyn in 1951. Her single panic attack occurred while she was in college. A friend took her to a Dyngus Day celebration (a Polish holiday the day after Easter Sunday) in Lockport, New York.

It was some sort of beer fest, with accordion music, polkas, etc. Very jolly, with some people tipsy. At one point, my heart was racing, and I broke out in a cold sweat. I was afraid I would be shot as part of the festivities—three quick shots in time to the polka.

Chaya never had Holocaust dreams, but in her waking life she is plagued by associations with the Holocaust.

I see images of the ovens and gas chambers in ordinary places. The garbage chute room in an apartment building I used to live in had one bare lightbulb hanging from the ceiling. It made me think of Auschwitz. I wouldn't take the garbage out if I could possibly help it. When I had to, I tried to stand as close to the door as possible, throw the garbage down the chute, and get out of there ASAP. Certain arched shapes make me think of the ovens. When I'm standing on a long line, whether at the post office, the bank, or Disney World, I obsess about standing in line to be gassed.

Often, panic attacks are set off by certain locations. A man born to a Jewish family in Johannesburg, South Africa, in 1960 says that he has panic attacks "when traveling to and in Germany." Betsy Ann Bloom, born to a Jewish family in Montgomery, Alabama, in 1956, went to Amsterdam for her junior year of college. Riding the train, she became so frightened that she fainted. Another Jewish woman, born in Cape Town, South Africa, was traveling on a train from Austria to Paris. At the French border, there was a knock on her compartment door, and the passengers were asked to produce their passports. She had a full-fledged panic attack.

Isaac Bekerman, born to a Jewish family in Colombia, South America, in 1950, had Holocaust survivors in his family. They discussed the Holocaust every day, which could account for the recurring nightmare he had from the age of nine until sixteen. At the age of sixty-four, Isaac visited Theresienstadt. Compared to the death camps where Jews were systematically murdered, Theresienstadt, where 35,440 Jews died of disease, was the "best" of the concentration camps. It was used by the Third Reich as a showcase to dupe the International Red Cross (after setting up fake stores, a coffee house, a bank, a school, and more, and planting flower gardens).

Yet it was in Theresienstadt and not in the other camps he toured that Isaac had a panic attack. "I could not even breath. I collapsed and cried. It took me four hours to return to normal."

Elka Ginsburg Caplan, who was born in the Bronx, New York, in 1940, had a panic attack when she was traveling in Europe with her husband and children. Due to a mix-up with their hotel reservations, they ended up driving through a corner of Germany and staying in a bed-and-breakfast. The owner of the house "had a Nazi symbol on his arm. He told us that he had been a Nazi prisoner in the States. Also, he remarked about my son's Magen David. I acted like a crazy woman. I was so panicked that I pushed the dresser in front of the door and all the suitcases behind the dresser. I didn't sleep a wink that night."

Judith Yael was born in New York in 1947. Her family was "nominally Jewish," but in her early twenties she rejected Judaism due to her theological questions about the Holocaust. "How could there even be a God who would let this happen?" Her spiritual search led her through agnosticism, then Hinduism, then messianic Christianity, and finally to a new understanding of Judaism. She is presently an Orthodox Jew.

When traveling in Europe after college, Judith, despite her strong feelings against everything German, had to pass through Germany to get to Denmark. Her traveling companion took ill, and they were detained in Germany overnight. Although the people around them were not threatening, Judith had a panic attack. Judith also had other indications of a past life in the Holocaust:

> Growing up, I was obsessed with the Holocaust. I read everything I could about it. At the age of twelve, I was so incredibly disturbed by the diary of Anne Frank that I even contacted her father, Otto Frank. I kept this obsession secret from everyone since I felt so weird.
>
> A few years ago, at a Holocaust remembrance event, I saw a photo of two terrified young women and a little girl about five years old, who was half hiding behind one of them. Close to them and facing them were two German officers laughing. One of them was pointing a raised pistol. I was mesmerized, and I could not move from there. It all felt so familiar.

Sometimes the German language triggers a panic attack. Efrat was born in Tel Aviv in 1972. At the age of twenty-four, she made a trip to Canada. Tour buses were taking tourists from various countries to a popular tourist spot. Then the unexpected occurred. The organizer of each bus called out to the people who had registered for it in their own language. When German was called out, Efrat had a panic attack. She was sure they were shouting *"Juden raus!"* (Jews, out!). The fear stayed with her until the end of the day. "I didn't enjoy the trip, even though it was something I had been looking forward to."

For Gregory Segal, born to a Jewish family in Johannesburg in 1965, his panic attacks have a unique trigger: pictures of female SS guards. The first time it happened he was on his computer. "I saw pictures of female SS guards and had a total panic attack. I felt like I was going to be ill, and immediately ran from the screen of my computer. To this day, I cannot look at images of female guards without having a panic attack."

At the age of four, Greg developed a phobia. Whenever his mother took him to visit certain friends who had an imitation log fire, he would scream uncontrollably and beg his mother to take him home. His mother could not understand his strange behavior and demanded that he stop it, but to no avail. Greg's parents sent him to psychologists, but no one could determine the source of his extreme fear of log fires.

> Years went by, and I started having dreams about being a female in a concentration camp, observing from the top of a hill the brutality happening below of female guards whipping prisoners. I woke up in a cold sweat. The dreams repeated themselves for

several weeks, then stopped. However, they left me with a curiosity as to why I had these experiences.

I actually think I was at the Płaszów concentration camp for two reasons. The first is my dream looking down from a big hill to a camp below looks like pictures I have seen of this camp. The second is because I read that there was a mass grave on top of the hill, where people were shot into a pit where a log fire was kept burning in order to dispose of the bodies.

A déjà vu experience is much subtler than a flashback or a panic attack. In a déjà vu, a person upon encountering a place or person for the first time feels an inexplicable sense of familiarity. Psychiatrist and *New York Times* bestselling author Dr. Judith Orloff, who is an assistant clinical professor of psychiatry at UCLA, wrote: "I describe many theories to explain déjà vu: a memory of a dream, a precognition, a coincidental overlapping of events, or even a past-life experience in which we rekindle ancient alliances."[29]

A déjà vu can be fleeting or dogged. For Andrew, born in South Africa in 1961, it was life-changing.

Raised in a secular Jewish family in Cape Town, Andrew never even heard of the Holocaust until he was fifteen years old. That year his parents transferred him to a Jewish school.

---

29. Judith Orloff, MD, "The Meaning of Déjà Vu," *Psychology Today,* April 16, 2010, https://www.psychologytoday.com/us/blog/emotional-freedom/201004/the-meaning-d-j-vu.

During a trip to Israel that same year, Andrew toured Meah Shearim, the starkest Chassidic neighborhood in Jerusalem. Andrew, with his long hair, jeans, and T-shirt, for the first time encountered Chassidic Jews with sidelocks and beards, wearing long black frock coats or knickers with white stockings. "I felt like I had 'come back home' and never wanted to leave," Andrew remembers.

Upon his return to South Africa, Andrew taught himself how to keep kosher and observe Shabbat, adopting—or he would say reclaiming—the identity of the Chassidic Jews he had encountered in Meah Shearim.

> I never felt part of my secular family at all. My real family was in the shtetl. My real friends were long-lost yeshivah students, my role models were Chassidic rebbes I read about and saw in photos. For my whole childhood I felt adopted; I never fit or belonged to where I was living, both in my family and country. I shared none of their values or interests.
>
> I had my own, very different identity and inner life, even though I was raised completely secular, and my parents fought my efforts to become religious for a long time.

Once he found out about the Holocaust, Andrew became obsessed with the subject. Immersed in Holocaust literature and photos, he experienced another déjà vu.

> When looking at pictures of Jews getting ready to be shot, in a forest on an overcast, cloudy day, I always felt like I was in the pictures, part of the

scenarios. I could stare into the pictures for hours, studying every detail, feeling what was going on. I felt like I was re-observing myself and my family and friends from long ago. Cloudy, rainy days always made me feel like I was somewhere other than at home or at school—I was really in a forest with my real townspeople, cold, hungry and waiting for something to happen. I totally identified with everyone I read about and saw in photos, even though I was thousands of miles away and decades apart.

A few years ago, I abandoned everything I had— my job, my home, my students, my friends—I left everything and moved across the United States, where I was then living, to take care of a ninety-one-year-old Auschwitz survivor I had met. Everyone told me I was completely crazy, but I felt absolutely driven to do that, and I never second-guessed or regretted my decision. I felt that I had to pay the Nazis back by caring for one of their victims. For me, it was very personal.

The sense of being "at home" in a foreign place may indicate a past life. Dr. Ian Fowler is a psychiatrist born to an Anglican family in Australia in 1961. After completing his studies at the University of London in the 1980s, he was touring Europe when he arrived in Berlin. He had a strange sensation there. "I knew the city," he marveled. "I didn't need to use a road map! I felt at home in Berlin. I had never felt so at home anywhere else. My direct ancestors can be traced back to 1667 in

London, but I never felt that kind of connection in London like I did in Berlin."

In February 2017, Dr. Fowler was touring Israel. In Jerusalem, he visited the Great Synagogue, where an exhibit of volumes of the Talmud were on display. Upon seeing the Talmud for the first time in this life, he had an extreme emotional reaction. As he recalls, "I burst into overwhelming sobs of joy and great sadness. I said, 'They didn't destroy them! They didn't destroy them! We survived!' I couldn't stop sobbing for some time."

Ally was born in Scotland in 1980. On her mother's side she is descended from Jews who came first to Ireland, then Scotland, to escape the Nazi regime. They converted to Catholicism in Ireland. Her family never discussed the Holocaust. Ally used to work in finance and is currently a stock trader. She has a phobia of tall men with short blond hair and blue eyes. "They send chills up my spine."

At the age of twenty-seven, Ally went to Poland with her sister and some friends for a girls' weekend. In Kraków, she got a very strong sense of déjà vu.

> I knew exactly where I was in the town (even though I'd never been there before), and I knew that the town square was around the corner from where I was standing. In that moment I saw the town square like I was back in the 1930s or '40s, and then I immediately recalled a dream I had about walking around the town square and some of the buildings within it. As I walked to the town square (in real time/present day) after experiencing the déjà vu, I

recognized some of the older buildings and felt like I was "home." It was then that I knew I was definitely a Holocaust victim and had been in Poland in my previous life. It was a very powerful experience.

During the holiday we had the chance to visit Auschwitz, but I couldn't go. It felt too close to me. My friends went, and I stayed in Kraków while they visited the place.

Approximately ten years ago, I heard a piece of opera/classical music on the radio. It immediately resonated with me, and I burst into tears. I took a note of the name of this powerful composition and decided to buy it. After the CD arrived, I discovered that the composition was about the Holocaust, with lyrics gleaned from writing left on a wall by a young female prisoner in Auschwitz. The name of the composition is *Symphony of Sorrowful Songs* by Górecki. I was astonished to discover the meaning behind this piece of music that had affected me so deeply.

At the conclusion of my online survey, Ally added: "PS: Please don't disbelieve me. It took a lot for me to do this tonight. This is not something I ever talk about, purely because most people aren't open-minded enough to believe in such things.... I know what's in my soul, though."

Sometimes the déjà vu of a place is associated with the physical sensations that may have occurred to the person in that place. Jan was born to a Jewish family in Chicago in 1974.

> This is very odd, but I think I may have been from Vienna. I visited the city about ten years ago in May, and the entire time I was there, I was freezing cold, so badly that my bones were physically aching. I can't explain the feeling.... I'd never been so cold and chilled before in my life, and I haven't been that cold ever since. It wasn't a virus, so my only explanation that made sense to me is reincarnation.
>
> I should mention that my trip to Vienna was the last stop on an Eastern European vacation that included a tour of Auschwitz. I was moved by Auschwitz, but for some reason it was Vienna that unsettled me more.

Laura Dwyer, born in Australia in 1966 to a Christian family, has a phobia of "enclosed spaces with low ceilings with one way in." She states:

> Our local slaughterhouse has a peaked roof that can be seen from the road, and for years it made me feel ill without knowing why. Then I saw a picture of Auschwitz, where the trains entered the complex, and I realized why the peaked roof made me feel like that.

A Jewish woman born in New York City in 1947 was seven years old when she saw Holocaust footage on television. "The scene was bulldozers shoveling the bones and dead corpses in the camps. I began crying hysterically, crying to my mother that I was there. She tried to reassure me that our family had never been in Germany. But I knew that I had been there."

A woman born to a Christian family in Bristol, UK, converted to Judaism in 1964 at the age of thirty-six. She had a déjà vu experience while sewing a decorative Jewish star on a banner for a synagogue in Los Angeles in 2001. "I had a profound feeling," she relates, "that this was not the first time I had sewn two yellow triangles together to make a Jewish star."

Ellen was born to a Protestant family in Lorain, Ohio, in 1954. "As much as I love forests," she writes, "whenever I see a grove of pines, my mind takes me to a place where people were slaughtered in the pine grove. As much as I want to relax and enjoy the peace of the breeze blowing through the pines, I cannot. I have a feeling that something horrible could happen in that setting."

When Ellen was living in Montreal as an adult, one day she was riding a bus and saw someone reading a Hebrew newspaper. "I started to panic, and the thought that went through my mind was, *They'll know you're Jewish!*"

Toby Klein Greenwald is a theater producer and director. She was born to a Jewish family in Cleveland in 1949. While growing up, Toby attended a summer camp where they sometimes sang Hebrew songs.

> I didn't understand any of the words, but there was one song I connected to the most, very deeply. I considered it "my song." I found out later it was the song of the partisans. When I visited the Holocaust

museum in Washington in my early fifties, I was standing in one of the halls and felt myself drawn like a magnet to the forest scene at the end of the hall. As I got closer, I heard the partisan song and saw that the forest scene was a tribute to the partisans. It mesmerized me.

A Jewish woman born in Chicago in 1951 traveled to Poland with her husband.

In Auschwitz, I felt totally on familiar ground. When we arrived at Auschwitz, we stood on the train platform. Books always describe Mengele in front of the little house and the train pulling up in such a way that the selection went to the gas chambers or the camp. When I stood on the train platform, I felt a different experience. I asked the guide about this discrepancy. He verified that indeed sometimes Mengele stood on the other side and made the selection opposite. I felt that I had been on the opposite side.

Sandra Wharton was born to a Jewish family in Oak Park, Illinois, in 1942.

I was in Greece once on a tour bus with monks sitting behind me speaking in German. I do not speak German, but at that time in my life could better understand Yiddish. They were looking for a post box, and I turned around and spoke to them in fluent, perfectly accented German. They would not believe I was not German or that I did not grow up speaking German. I was never able to speak German again.

I went to Eastern Europe with UJA [the United Jewish Appeal] from Chicago, and we visited Czechoslovakia, Austria, Romania, Poland, and East and West Germany. We had, as a group, all traveled to Israel previously. I was never uncomfortable anywhere other than Austria, which still strikes me as strange. I remember sitting in the hotel lobby in Vienna, looking at the staircase and getting the chills. I did not want to be there.

I felt strongly that I knew where I was, and I was not comfortable from the second we arrived until we left. I still get a bad feeling even now when I think about it, and there is no way I would want to return. We visited many concentration camps and met with many survivors, but nothing affected me as strongly as my time in Vienna. After my experience in Vienna, I thought I would abhor Berlin, but that was not the case.

For as long as I can remember, I've had nightmares where I wake up screaming. In the nightmares there are very clean buildings (maybe four or five stories high max) along a beautiful waterway. The waterway is raging, and I am running in the opposite direction of the raging water. I am caught by men in uniform, and then I wake up screaming, "Help, help!" It never goes any further.

In the last few years, I still have the same night

experiences, but previously it was several times a week and now it is just occasionally.

Because flashbacks are caused by trauma, sometimes the fear and anguish of the trauma lingers long after the flashback ceases, like a persistent drizzle after a thunderstorm. Some souls are sodden with their Holocaust memories.

Such is the case of Regina, born to a Christian family in California in 1973. She had a recurring nightmare that, according to her parents, started when she was two or three years old. Regina says that it's always the same dream, and over forty years later it continues to haunt her nights. She speaks German and Dutch in her sleep.

During the day she often has flashbacks to the same past life as the child in the Netherlands she sees in her dreams, a coherent autobiography of horror. In these flashbacks, she sees that when the Nazis were rounding up the Jews of Holland, her parents decided that she, the youngest child in her family and the only blonde, could pass for an Aryan and thus survive. On the day of the roundup, they hid her in a chest in the home of a Christian neighbor. She never saw her family again, leaving her bereft—and guilty. "They had to go to their deaths alone," Regina cries, as tears eighty years blocked are finally allowed to flow.

The Christian neighbor belonged to the Dutch underground. By the time she was thirteen years old, Regina was working as a messenger for the underground. Naturally, her life was fraught with danger and fear, especially the dread that a single mistake of hers could doom her cohort to death. Near the end of the war, the Nazis discovered her underground network and tortured and killed all of them.

In recent years Regina's flashbacks and nightmares have become harder to bear. Two years after first contacting me, Regina wrote:

> Things are very difficult here, with very detailed nightmares that contain knowledge I should not have. As I have said, I've had Holocaust nightmares in German since I was three. It was the same one over and over. But now I speak German out loud all night and have these precise dreams.... They are each very different scenarios, getting more brutal and more detailed, and when I do the research they are far too accurate for things I should not know about. It is unbearable.

The story of Caron Levy, born to a Jewish family in South Africa in 1961, includes flashbacks, panic attacks, and phobias. Caron is a speech pathologist and educator, and for many years was a lecturer at the University of the Witwatersrand, the biggest university in South Africa. The Holocaust besieged her mind at the age of eleven with nightmares and waking visions of concentration camps, and has never let it go. When awake, she sees women in bunks in barracks. "My place seemed to be near an opening, as I see the light of the sun coming in always."

Throughout her adult life, she had "an unnatural pull to Poland. Not a love—certainly not, but an inner knowledge of the place—the forests and the vastness." In 2012, she took what she calls "a personal odyssey to Poland." She visited Auschwitz-Birkenau and Majdanek, where she was moved as any feeling person would be. When visiting Treblinka, however, she had a panic attack, and became frozen to the spot.

> I couldn't leave that space. The tour guide was yelling for me to get back onto the bus, but I just could not leave that place. Finally, I walked backwards out of the site. It was awful...like I belonged there. I didn't talk much on the trip, and for one year exactly after the trip I didn't have one dream. As soon as a year had passed, the dreams and flashbacks and phobias started again. And still continue.

During Caron's recurrent panic attacks, she feels queasiness in her stomach, sweats, and is gripped by fear. Her triggers are icy weather and fasting (as on the Jewish fast day of Yom Kippur).

> The cold and the hunger. That is something that never leaves me. It flits through my mind when we have a cold day, and the thought flashes through my mind of how cold we were, with no respite.
>
> When I look at the peels of fruits and vegetables, I get quite distressed, as I know that those peels would have made a broth that could have saved lives.
>
> The bottom line here is really this: The Holocaust never leaves me. It's an unnatural state of mind. It never leaves me. I see shadowy gray people walking on gravel, always in groups and starving and cold.

Little wonder that psychiatrists Brian Weiss and Ian Stevenson and Jungian analyst Sabine Lucas maintain that some cases of panic attacks and anxiety simply cannot be cured without dealing with past lives. Perhaps someday soon psychology devoid of the knowledge of past lives will be regarded like medical science devoid of the knowledge of viruses.

CHAPTER 6

MYSTERIOUS FEARS AND PHOBIAS

THROUGHOUT MY LIFE I HAVE HAD A STRANGE PHOBIA—a fear of falling. Not a fear of heights. I love looking down from the top of the Empire State Building. Rather, I fear falling from the ground down. While hiking, when I reach a stream that must be forded by stepping from one stone to another, even if the stones are only a few inches apart, I stand frozen at the bank until someone grasps my hand and helps me across. My rational mind screams, *So what if you fall? The water is only six inches deep!* But the rest of my mind swirls in vertigo, deaf to reason, immune to courage. It's not the water I fear. It's the act of falling.

The first time I went to Yad Vashem, the pictures that most horrified me, which entered me not through the aperture in my eyes but through a hole in my heart, were the photos of the Einsatzgruppen. These were the German mobile killing squads that lined up Jews along pits and shot them so that they fell into the pits—murder and burial with a single bullet, the ultimate in German efficiency. While I had a flashback in Vienna (described in the prologue), I never had dreams or flashbacks of ghettos, trains, concentration camps, or gas chambers. Intuitively I knew that I never experienced these telltale signs of a Holocaust incarnation because my previous life had followed a different path. Like 1,150,000 other Jews, I was led out to a local forest and killed by the German soldiers and their collaborators, who fired at me and my children. I fell into a pit. Thus, my phobia of falling from the ground down.

Regular fears are like garments that you may outgrow. A phobia is like your skin. You can be cured of a phobia, but only with deliberate therapy or the release of the trauma that caused it, as described in some of the cases below.

A rabbi, the head of an Israeli yeshivah, went to therapist Efim Svirsky to cure him of a bothersome phobia. He was afraid of showers. He had no problem with baths, and he enjoyed swimming in the ocean or a pool, but he dreaded taking a shower. Svirsky assumed he had had a childhood trauma connected to a shower, so he put him into a state of deep relaxation and asked him to go to the first time he had experienced a shower as frightening. The rabbi found himself in the gas chambers. Svirsky guided him through his death, telling him to "go up with the soul." The rabbi saw himself going out of his body and into the spiritual realms. When he returned to his normal consciousness, he expressed surprise. He did not believe in reincarnation. Some days later, he informed Svirsky that his phobia of showers had vanished.

In order to lure their victims to their death, the Nazis told their prisoners that they were going to the showers. They were told to undress and fold their clothes neatly for after the shower. The gas chambers themselves were fitted with shower heads. Only when the doors were sealed shut and Zyklon B gas came out instead of water did the people inside, choking for air, know the true nature of the "showers."

It is thus little wonder that many of my survey respondents reported a phobia of showers. One successful entertainer wrote to me: "I can't get into the shower without moaning for five minutes."

Rebecca, born to a Jewish family in Miami in 1978, reported: "As a child we had a small shower near the kitchen that for some reason reminded me of a gas chamber. I was petrified of showering there, fearing something other than water would come out. It was completely illogical."

Every survey respondent who reported a phobia also reported Holocaust-related dreams, panic attacks, or additional phobias. The scars of the Holocaust are holistic. Thus, a man born in Denmark to Swedish and German parents, in addition to his fear of showers, had a dream that recurred from the age of four until thirty-two: "I had vivid dreams about me and my brother Adam hiding alone from the Nazis." The entertainer quoted above also had a fear of losing children. So great was her fear that she never allowed her children to go on school trips.

This phobia of the loss of children was reported by many of my respondents. Juliana was born into a Christian family in Brazil in 1983. She first learned about the Holocaust when her family moved to Europe when she was eleven years old, but she started dreaming Holocaust-like nightmares years before that, when she was only five or six. In addition, Juliana suffers from a phobia: "My phobia is to lose my kids or that they might be taken away from me."

Daniella was born to a Jewish family in Brooklyn. Her fears center on her children:

> I always think of where I can hide in my house or build a secret room. I keep my passports updated. I am not much into jewelry, but I think it's important for Jews to have jewelry so that they can sell it quickly and leave.
>
> I read *Mila 18* and *Exodus* [both by Leon Uris], and the scenes of the Warsaw Ghetto seemed to connect with me. Particularly the underground bunkers where they had the children's hospital. I always felt like I was there. After my first son was born, I had postpartum depression that involved many nightmares about the Holocaust. (This happened with all my other children as well.)
>
> When my first son was about eighteen months old, my husband and I were watching a Holocaust movie, where a young couple with a child who was about two years old got on a train. I was totally shaken up. After that I refused to watch or read anything about the Holocaust.
>
> Every time my kids were sick as toddlers and they were feverish, I would have nightmares that I didn't

have medicine for them and that they were suffering and I couldn't do anything about it. I feel as if I
lost a young child in the Warsaw Ghetto to illness. I
am tearing up as I write this.

The most poignant and detailed account of the dread
of losing children is the story of Allison, who was born to a
Jewish family in South Carolina in 1968. Allison grew up in
the Deep South, moving to various cities as her father's job
demanded.

I knew growing up that there was a very distinct
chance that people could come to my classroom
and ask the other kids to point out where the Jews
were. I waited for that to happen. I never trusted
the other kids. Whenever we moved to a new
house, I would check where the hiding places were
or where the escape routes were. I remember doing
that even as a very small child. I thought that everyone else did that. As an adult, I found out that that
was not normal.

There was no Holocaust education, but I knew
about it. We didn't have survivors in our synagogue;
I never heard it discussed. At bat mitzvah time
when I was twelve, they started talking about it in
pop culture, but I already knew about it. When I
saw pictures, I recognized them. The first few times
I encountered [the Holocaust], I already knew very
much about it. No one had to explain it to me. I knew
what had happened and how it had happened. It
was something I just knew about.

As an adult, I was very afraid of a lot of things, especially when I had children. If I said goodbye to my children when they went to school, I was afraid I would never see them again. If I left them with a babysitter, I was afraid I would be separated from them. So I almost never left them with a babysitter. I was always overprotective and anxious.

When my children were little, we made a trip to Israel. One day I was sitting alone on a bench in the Jewish Quarter of Jerusalem's Old City waiting to meet a friend. An English-speaking woman sat down next to me. Out of nowhere, she started telling me about her experiences in the Shoah. She had been married and lived in Germany with her husband and two little boys. They came and took her husband one day. A week later they came and took away the children, who were one and four years old. She did nothing to stop them. As they carried her son away, he cried over the Nazi's shoulder, "But Mommy, you'll make me breakfast tomorrow?" After that, she made no effort to survive. She had no interest in living, but she did.

At the end of the war, in a DP camp, she met a man and married him and had four children with him. They lived in New Jersey. She never loved her second husband or her children with him. She hoped every day that God would take her and she would die.

At this point in the woman's narrative, my friend showed up, so I left. I have no idea why this complete stranger told me her story. She told me that she had never told anyone else her story. I don't know why she told it to me. There was no context for it. I had not asked her for her story. Yet in subsequent years, I couldn't speak about that conversation without breaking down completely.

A year ago, I was reading something online. Someone had written in a question to Quora.com. People post interesting questions there, usually about academic topics, and experts can answer them. One day someone posted a picture of Jews being processed in a concentration camp. There were two guards and thousands of Jews. The question was: Why didn't the Jews fight back?

Several people posted historical and sociological responses. One person explained it in such a way that he walked you through what you would have seen or experienced as you were arriving at the train platform. As I was reading his description, I had a very strong flashback of being there. It was triggered by the statement: "When the crematoria were on, they produced so much debris in the air that it actually obscured the sun."

I found myself reliving that experience as the viewer. There was no sound associated with it. Getting off a train onto the platform, I was wearing a coat. I had no suitcase or anything with me. You could still see the sun, but a lot of things were floating around in front of the sun. It was very cold. I realized at that point that I knew what had

happened to my family when I saw what was floating in the air.

That was enough. All of a sudden, it made sense
to me. I was afraid to know more because the feeling that I had was that I had probably done something very bad to survive. I had a distinct sense
that I didn't want to know, that it shouldn't bleed
over into this life. But I was not successful. I was
suffering and causing other people to suffer from
not coming to terms with what had happened in
that life. I was increasing the damage instead of
limiting it.

At that point, I had to really think about whether I was nuts. I had no history of mental illness, but
it was just an odd thing to believe that I had lived
before, that I had actually been in the Holocaust.
It doesn't really match with the rest of my belief
system. I'm not a spiritual person. This wasn't being transmitted to me by aluminum foil antennae.
On the other hand, the idea that I had been in the
Holocaust wasn't shocking to me. It was just like
something I had always known.

So I did some online research for reincarnation
and the Holocaust. I found Yonassan Gershom, and
read his book,[30] and I decided that if I'm crazy, there
are a lot of other people equally crazy.

Then I got in touch with Carol Bowman, author of
Children's Past Lives. She too believes that she was

---

30. Rabbi Yonassan Gershom's *Beyond the Ashes* (Virginia Beach: *A.R.E. Press*, 1992)
was the first book published on this subject.

in the Holocaust. She lives outside Philadelphia. I flew to Philadelphia for an appointment with her.

During my session with Carol, I reexperienced my past. I had been a young adult, married, in Poland. I had two small boys. Like the woman on the bench, I had given them over to the Nazis without any attempt to hide or flee or anything. They had us all registered. They had a day that they said that we had to go to the square and bring them.[31] So, I went, and lined up with everyone, and handed my children to the Nazis on the truck. Unlike the people who were brave or who hid, I did absolutely nothing at all. The worst part of it for me was that I was relieved to do it, because I didn't want to watch them be killed. The most cowardly act you could imagine.

My husband had told me to keep them safe. Either he was away or he was trying to get us out, but we waited too long. I didn't want to be poor. [Before being imprisoned in the ghetto] I had my house and my stuff, and I didn't want to leave everything behind. I went along till the last second, just pretending that everything would be fine. I did not see my husband again. He had asked me to keep the children safe, and I didn't.

---

31. This must have been in the Lodz Ghetto, the second-largest ghetto in Europe after the Warsaw Ghetto. On September 4, 1942, Chaim Rumkowski, the head of the *Judenrat*, demanded that the Jews turn over their children for deportation as the only way of surviving. Many families tried to hide their children or committed collective suicide.

I ended up in a camp, but I didn't last long. I just laid down and died. I remember being undressed and cold. I was angry. The Jewish community I was in had told me that if we were compliant with them, we'd be safe. We just had to do what they said. By that time, I don't think I was all there.

This was all stuff that Carol Bowman didn't know. She just asked me questions. For all I know this is all imaginary, but it didn't feel that way to me. I think if I was going to imagine something, I would imagine being a better person than that.

This is the chilling background of Allison's phobia of losing her children. In this lifetime, she has the feeling that her husband and two of her children are the same as her husband and children in the Polish lifetime. She is involved in an ongoing struggle to act differently—and better—this time around.

Not surprisingly, a phobia of trains was common among my respondents. Samantha, born in Boulder, Colorado, in 1985, wrote: "As a very young child (age two), I was terrified of trains. I would scream at the sight of a toy train or a train on TV." Other respondents reported throwing tantrums as young children when they were supposed to get on a train.

Amelia Marks, born to a Jewish family in London in 1950, remembers:

I was very frightened of steam trains and particularly their sound. Once, I went into an exhibition in which there was a video set up to repeat—like in a loop. The video showed views out of a train moving along tracks in the country, not very fast. The sound of the rails on the tracks was so disturbing that I had to leave the room. I had such a sense of foreboding and fright. I tried several times to return to the room with the video, but it had the same effect on me each time.

Sharon, born to a Jewish family in South Africa in 1960, reported:

I had this strange phobia of trains, not the electrical kind, only the ones that had a sound of *clickety-clack*. Even if I never saw the train and just heard that sound, I was filled with fear. When I was a little girl, my sister and I went to stay with an aunt and uncle for a few days and they took us on a short trip on such a train. It was terrible for me, and I remember thinking that I was going to my death. I never verbalized my fear of these trains until I was approximately eighteen years old, and then just to one or two friends. I just made a comment in passing, as I didn't want anyone to think that I was "strange."

People who start to suspect that their dreams, flashbacks, or phobias derive from a previous life in the Holocaust have one of two reactions. Some, like Allison, question their own sanity and search for external confirmation that their suspicions may indeed be true. Others, like Goldie, who was born to a Jewish family in Toledo, Ohio, in 1957, have a strong internal confidence in the truth of their intuitive feelings. When as a youth Goldie started learning about the Holocaust, she recognized it as her authentic past. As she wrote to me:

> I just identified totally with it, to the point that I cried and cried and screamed, "I can't go through this again!" Wow, was I shocked when I did that! I read everything I could, over and over again. It was *my* story.
>
> Until I read your article, I never knew that anyone else felt like this. But that didn't matter, because I felt this was true for me. It didn't matter how weird it was. About this, I never had any doubt, and don't need anybody to accept it. It's my story. I know it.

Some of my respondents professed a phobia of Germans—people with blond hair and blue eyes—and the German language. Angela Lopez, whose dream and panic attack is recorded in chapter 3, was born in 1966 in Brooklyn to a Catholic family, her mother Italian and her father Puerto Rican. From her childhood, she had an aversion to German-looking people.

> When I was a young girl (about six), my mother had a friend who had blond hair and blue eyes, and I remember not liking Susan simply due to her blond

hair. To this day I find the blue eyes scary, too devilish looking. I used to tell my mother, "Yucky Susan with her 'germy' hair is here." I don't know what made me refer to her hair in such a manner. To this day I still do not feel comfortable around people with those features, and I don't have any friends with blond hair or blue eyes.

Trudi Goodman, born to a Jewish family in Boston in 1954, as a child of six or seven played a strange game with her sister:

> If you were captured by Nazis, what would you do? Would you tell them you were Jewish? I took it as a matter of fact that I had two choices. If you didn't tell them, you could help others and of course stay alive. If you did say you were Jewish, then you could walk into the showers and comfort the frightened children who were going to die with you. It didn't faze me that I would die. I thought that was the honorable thing, to comfort the little children.

Trudi also professes a phobia of the German language. "I hate hearing people speak in German. It frightens me. I was working as a tour guide in Boston. I had Austrians on my tour. When they spoke among each other in Austrian German, they frightened me. I couldn't wait to get them off my tour. I hated them."

Rachel, whose dream of being an assimilated Viennese girl appears in chapter 4, recalls:

> In this life, I was born with an irrational fear of Germans and the German language. When I was

little, I had no exposure to Germans, and I had never met them. But when I was little, I would tell my mom they were evil murderers and that I was terrified of them. I was terrified of their language, their appearance—everything about them. Yet (at that point) I had never met Germans in this life, and this was before I even knew about the Holocaust. So there is no explanation for me knowing all about Germans and the German language and knowing they were murderers. I believed they would kill me in my sleep.

My parents confirmed that my beliefs about this seemingly came out of nowhere. They had never exposed me to the German language, yet I knew the language and it instilled great fear in me. I viewed Germans as monsters, and I feared them more than the "monster under the bed."

Rabbi Yonassan Gershom in his book *Beyond the Ashes* documents three cases of a phobia of black boots by non-Jewish American women born after World War II. He quotes a testimony from Donnie Ducharme from Raleigh, North Carolina:

I was born in June 1948 into a Southern Baptist family in North Carolina. As a child, I was very sickly until age six. During the early years I was petrified of black boots—the shiny kind that go up to the knees. My grandfather had a rubber pair, and I exhibited great fear about those boots. My mother would set them near the wood stove so that I wouldn't touch it and get burned. I never went near the stove because of the boots. I remember going around the perimeter of the room with my back against the wall—to get as far away from those boots as possible.

I never understood why I was afraid of the boots until I watched a movie about Hitler and saw the goose-steppers. There were those boots! I felt then that I had been there.[32]

A few of my survey respondents also reported a phobia of black boots. Lynn, born to a Jewish family in Philadelphia in 1954, wrote:

When I read reports about the children carving butterflies on the wooden bunks to give other children hope, I burst into tears and couldn't stop sobbing. I "knew" I was one of those "artists."... Seeing heavy black boots in early childhood greatly distressed me. My heart pounded, my palms sweated, and I lost all warmth and got a cold feeling. Today, I still get anxious seeing thick black boots.

Lynn's testimony is significant in that it pairs a sense of having been a child in the Holocaust with the phobia of black boots. Young children in the Holocaust were too small to look their persecutors in the face; they saw their boots.

---

32. Yonassan Gershom, *Beyond the Ashes: Cases of Reincarnation from the Holocaust* (Virginia Beach: A.R.E. Press, 1992), p. 131.

Brittany Broussard was born to a Catholic family in Louisiana in 1982. She suffers from claustrophobia, a common phobia, but in her case, it is accompanied by a Holocaust dream:

> I have always my entire life had dreams that I was hiding or running, always hiding from someone trying to kill me. I just had this dream that in no way could be anything else besides a memory of me being a twin or triplet. Three of us girls looked to be the same age or size for sure, at age three or four. I was hiding with our mother underground, under a home. She was constantly putting her finger over her mouth, reminding us to be quiet.
>
> One of us shrieked, and the door on the ceiling of our hiding place flew open. I kept looking between my mother and the soldiers. They were yelling. I would imagine it would have been very loud, but in my dream it went dead silent like out of fear. I saw my mother's face in complete terror while they grabbed her, and some came toward us. They shot me, and I woke up. In the dream I just knew we were Jewish, with dark hair, and our mother was the same. No one said anything, and I didn't notice the soldiers being Nazis, but I just knew. I'm convinced this is a memory and not just a dream. It was too real and makes no sense to be a dream.
>
> I'm extremely claustrophobic, and if I even imagine being in a two-door car in the back seat, or underground, my chest gets tight. When people mention underground bunkers for possible survival

for the future, I know I will gladly die before I hide underground.

Caron Levy, the South African academic and educator mentioned at the end of chapter 5, listed her phobias:

- I have an almost irrational fear of any kind of bureaucracy. Official buildings make me shiver in fear, and I cannot stand in line for anything. I have an almost physiological reaction to the above.

- The sight of the airport/train station causes an unexplained anxiety attack. My stomach reacts physically, and I shake uncontrollably.

- I also cannot be near any type of gas. This may not be related, but I will not install a gas stove, nor will I turn on gas heaters nor barbecues.

- The other strange phenomena that I have had to deal with throughout my life are dreams of camps and marches. My husband has commented that I often moan and shout while I'm sleeping.

- My fasting on Yom Kippur and Tishah B'Av is fraught with unnatural feelings of *So this is what "they" felt like with no food/water.* I mean—who thinks like that?

A common phobia described by my respondents is fear of lack of food, or sometimes fear of emaciated or very thin people. Although this phobia could be traced back to death by starvation in many places and periods, in all the cases below this phobia was accompanied by Holocaust dreams, flash-backs, or other Holocaust-related phobias.

Liat, born in Israel in 1984 to a Jewish family that had em-igrated from Europe two decades before the Holocaust, had recurrent childhood dreams and accompanying phobias. She has a fear of lack of food, and her mother told her that when she was only two years old she would hide food throughout the house.

> I had déjà vu experiences. I never visited Warsaw, but I recognize places there from pictures. The building from which I was murdered does not exist today. The wall [around the ghetto] doesn't exist anymore. But I clearly remember the building on the other side of the wall.
>
> On Holocaust Day [observed annually in Israel on the 27th of the Hebrew month of Nissan] when I was six years old, I turned off the television while my parents were in the middle of watching a doc-umentary about the Holocaust. My parents got angry at me. I told them that they would never understand what happened there, and it was a shame to waste their time trying to understand— as if I, a six-year-old child, understood!

Jeanette was born into an Anglican family in Sunderland, UK, in 1953. She testifies: "I have a terrible fear of not hav-ing enough food in the house. My cupboards are bulging. If I haven't got a huge amount of food, I get very anxious." This phobia is accompanied by a recurring dream:

> The first detailed dream that I can remember oc-
> curred when I was in my early teens, and I was sitting
> next to an icy river, in the snow, wearing nothing but
> a filthy blanket. I was bald and starved—all bones—
> and behind me there was a huge conflagration. I
> was exhausted and knew in my dream that I had
> walked many, many miles. Many years later I read
> about the "death marches." I had known about the
> camps, but not about the marches.

Miriam Schwartz, who was born to a Jewish family in
Brooklyn in 1951, always had a "food issue, not with what I
eat, but with limiting how much I eat. If you tell me I can't eat
a certain kind of food, like sugar, dairy, or wheat, that's okay.
But if you tell me that I have to limit quantities, that's hard for
me."

At the age of fifty, Miriam was suffering from mononucle-
osis. Someone suggested that she go to an energy healer near
her home in Jerusalem.

> I saw him several times for energy healing. This time
> I was lying on his table. He saw in a past life that I
> lived in Warsaw, in a comfortable family, that I was
> sixteen years old. He could see the lace tablecloth
> and Shabbat candlesticks. He said I had a good life
> and I was wanting for nothing. Then, as I was lying
> on the table, I started having these very strange
> physical experiences. I started feeling terrible low
> back pain. That passed. Then I felt that someone
> had carved a hole in my stomach, that it was totally

concave. Then I remember feeling very, very cold.

Afterwards he said to me that my physical feelings were from the starvation in the ghetto. I felt that that made sense to me. I had never, ever experienced something physical like that in my life.

Starvation. That's what I'm convinced happened. He said I would feel unburdened afterwards.

After this happened, I decided that I wanted to go to Yad Vashem. I wanted to go alone. I walked through the museum, read about the gas chambers, the crematoria, the trains…. Nothing really affected me until I got to the room of the Warsaw Ghetto. The bricks that the room was paved with were actually taken from the Warsaw Ghetto. The room has photographs. I read on a plaque that eighty thousand people died of starvation in the Warsaw Ghetto. I just dropped down on the floor and ran my hands over the floor. I was powerfully overtaken.

Driving home from Yad Vashem, it was as if a light bulb went off for me. I suddenly realized, *Oh my gosh, no wonder I have an issue with quantity of food. If I died of starvation, that's a normal reaction.*

Although the phobias above were each mentioned by several people, other phobias were idiosyncratic. For example, a woman born to a Protestant family in Tonbridge, Kent, who later converted to Judaism, has "a detestation of detached hair." Might she in her previous life have worked cutting hair off the women's corpses after they were removed from the gas chambers, part of the standard procedure at Auschwitz?

Another woman, born to a Jewish family in Cape Town, claimed a very specific phobia: "fear of German officers in black leather raincoats with glasses."

A Catholic woman born in Cleveland in 1955 reported that she had a phobia of having her hair cut off, accompanied by childhood dreams of having all her hair shaved off. Again, standard procedure in most concentration camps.

One of my respondents, Audrey Kashuk, born to a Jewish family in Denver in 1957, had a phobia of stripes, like the concentration camp uniforms in most camps.

> That is my issue. I cannot wear stripes—ever. I shudder when I see them.
>
> From the time I was a small child, I refused to wear stripes! I couldn't have anything with stripes. Not clothing or bedding or towels or anything. They absolutely flipped me out.
>
> I was obsessed from the age of eight or nine with survival skills. I would write sayings on a paper notepad with ideas I would contemplate on what it would take to survive. I posted them on my bedroom door. The door was filled from top to bottom with my sayings of survival. If I hear German, a language I had *zero* connection to growing up, I shiver and feel tremendous fear. The only language in our assimilated home was English—and a few of the basic Yiddish words that everyone grows up with.

I taught myself to stop remembering my dreams as a young girl because they were so frightening. Always a deathly chase and hiding. They were recurring and continued forward from one night to the next. At about age sixteen, I literally worked on shutting down my dreams and to this day do not remember them.

I had a date when I was about seventeen, and the young man picked me up in a Porsche. I refused to go with him, as I could not get into his car. I was repelled by all German automobiles—to this day.

Helen was born to a Jewish family in Brooklyn in 1953. She has a phobia about being discovered that she is a Jew, although whenever she moves to a new city, she feels more secure living in Jewish neighborhoods.

I had dreams related to the Holocaust. I don't remember how old I was when they started, but I do remember that while the scene was not always the same, the situation was. I was always with other people, and we all knew that Nazis were coming to kill us and there was nothing we could do about it. The fear was intense.

For many, many years I was terrified to keep the radio or television too loud when something "controversial" was on or when there was something explicitly Jewish on. I would turn the volume very low so that it could not be heard by anyone but myself—even when I lived alone. I would never put up a mezuzah or use Jewish words in the company of gentiles. If I picked up a Jewish newspaper or magazine from a public vendor and had to carry it in my hand, I would roll it up so that the front cover could not be seen.

The ghastliest phobia was related to me by therapist Efim Svirsky. A Russian-Israeli woman in her fifties came to him to help her alleviate her terrible phobia of rodents. He put her into a state of deep relaxation and asked her, "Where did this fear start?"

She went right back to the Holocaust. She saw herself as a young boy being taken with his mother and all the people in the village. The Germans led them to a ditch. When they told the people to undress, his mother hid him by piling all the clothes on top of him. The Germans shot everyone, then left. This little child got out from under the clothes and found himself alone in the forest. He started looking for his mother and jumped into the uncovered grave. He found his dead mother's body, and just lay next to her. When night fell, the rats came. He was killed by the rats.

Efim Svirsky took this patient through her death, guiding her to go up with her soul into the spiritual realms. Through that process, her terrible fear subsided.

A traumatic death leaves an ugly stain in the form of a phobia. Various therapies try various stain removers. The most effective stain remover is the consciousness that the stain adheres only to an external level of the psyche. The soul itself is ever pure. The stain, ugly as it is, is only on the garment.

CHAPTER 7

LIFTING THE VEIL: PAST-LIFE REGRESSIONS

Naomi, a twenty-nine-year-old opera singer living in London, was desperate to lose weight. Someone told her that hypnosis is effective for weight loss, so one day in 2011 Naomi went to Dr. Garfinkle, a respected hypnotherapist. She didn't tell him that as a young child she'd had repeated nightmares where she would try to scream but no voice would emerge, and she would wake up with heart palpitations. She didn't tell him that as a teenager every night she'd had nightmares of the Holocaust. She didn't tell him that when she traveled through Germany, especially when driving past forests, she saw dead bodies in the woods. All she told Dr. Garfinkle was that she wanted to be hypnotized to lose weight.

Within minutes I was under, falling into a ditch holding somebody's hand. I was tall, skinny, undressed, with shaved head. I landed onto other bodies and mud. I was sandwiched between other bodies. My neck had cracked or broken. I tried to scream Shema, but no one could hear me. My neck really hurt. It was twisted to the left. I shed tears and more tears. There was the smell of mud. I was choked.

The hypnotist woke me up from that to a safe place. I was so ill for the rest of the week.

I went to see him a second time. When I went under, I experienced it all over again, all in the same way. But this time I could scream Shema. I screamed his living room down with Shema!!! So loud!!!! I could feel my body just expanding.

I went home, sad, crying, deflated, but since then, I haven't had a single nightmare of the Holocaust. I have always read whatever I could get my hands on about the Holocaust, but since that hypnosis session, when I read Holocaust memoirs, I have not felt the sadness in the same way. I don't feel choked after reading them. My body, or perhaps my soul, just accepts what has happened.

Getting hypnotized was the best thing I did. It provided some sort of closure, and healing. I am so grateful to Dr. Garfinkle, an elderly man, who made it safe for me to express. I shed so many tears with him, I could feel my body just expanding.

In this lifetime, I sing opera. I feel that my neck breaking in that previous life, so that I couldn't

even say Shema out loud, needed to be healed so I
could be heard again. For me, the voice is all about
healing.

There are three different types of PLR (past-life regressions).
The first is when someone such as a Kabbalist, psychic, energy
healer, or clairvoyant tells someone else who he or she was in
a previous lifetime. This chapter contains none of this type of
PLR. Although several of my respondents cited such an experience as a validation of their own nightmares, panic attacks, and
so on, I have chosen not to use them because the identification
of a past life did not originate in the respondents themselves.

The second type is through hypnosis or deep relaxation
guided by a trained therapist, who facilitates the mind's entering into a light trance. The therapist then asks open-ended
questions, such as "When did this phobia first start?" or "Look
around you. What do you see?" or "What are you wearing?" In
PLR hypnosis, the subject sees or knows what is happening in
that past life, while at the same time the subject is conscious
of who and where he is in the present life.

Contrary to popular misconception, the subject's free will
and conscience are not suspended during hypnosis. Hypnosis
allows the mind to access unconscious memories, from this
life and past lives. In the hypnotic state, the mind is more
susceptible to suggestion (e.g., to stop smoking), which is
why some hypnotherapists have been accused of implanting
"memories" that did not exist. Since past-life regressionists
have no particular agenda, they ask only open-ended questions and make no suggestions.

The third type of PLR is self-induced, through either meditation or various techniques of self-hypnosis. Self-induced PLR can also come spontaneously, when something triggers the memory, or during meditation when the meditator enters into an alpha state. Spontaneous PLR sometimes occurs in children between the ages of three and seven, as seen in the case of the Finnish boy Teuvo Koivisto described in this chapter. A PLR can also be induced deliberately, using techniques taught in workshops or online.

Dr. Brian Weiss, Chairman Emeritus of Psychiatry at the Mount Sinai Medical Center in Miami, has given workshops to thousands of people, teaching them the techniques of PLR, and also offers CDs of guided meditations and regressions. The following fascinating PLR was experienced using a YouTube guided self-hypnosis audio.

The case of Kati Andersson is extraordinary not only because she discovered a non-Jewish past life in the Holocaust, but also because she found independent verification of her PLR. Katie was born to a Catholic family in Naples, Florida, in 1981. Unlike almost all of my other respondents, Katie had no Holocaust dreams as a child nor as an adult. As an undergraduate at the University of Colorado, Katie, who majored in art, did drawings of Holocaust concentration camp inmates that won awards and were praised for their emotion and "accuracy," although she never used a visual reference.

Asked whether she has phobias, Katie replied: "Absolute terror and preoccupation with losing my home, my family, and everything. There is nothing that has happened to me in this life that explains my fears." Katie's only behavioral peculiarity is her compulsion to work, and to not eat until she has finished her project. This compulsion to work without eating led Katie, while in graduate school at the Smithsonian's Decorative Arts program, to a nervous breakdown, although psychiatrists determined that she did not have OCD nor anorexia.

While in her twenties, Katie was involved in a relationship that she intuited was dangerous. For her "protection," she decided to do something totally uncharacteristic: She got a tattoo. She was very specific about what kind of tattoo she wanted: on the inside of her left forearm, in white ink so it would not be noticed by others, and just the letter Z.

At the age of thirty-seven, Katie was taking care of her dying mother in Florida. A friend, Tina, suggested that she go for a past-life regression, but Katie could not leave her mother alone. So Tina sent her a link for a YouTube guided PLR that she could do at home. Katie had never done anything like this before. She expected that she might go back to an ancient lifetime, but was surprised by what she indeed saw.

> It was dawn. I was standing in a field with trees around it. I knew that it was the last day of my life. There had been something there that had been destroyed. The audio voice asked, "What are you wearing?" I looked down at my clothes. They were not from an ancient period. They were twentieth-century pants, caked in mud, and stiff. I looked down at my shoes, and I knew they were someone else's shoes. I was a man. I wasn't expecting that either.
>
> The audio voice asked what I looked like. When I saw my face, my cheekbones were sunken, my eyes

were sunken in, and there was no color in my skin. I looked like a dead man walking.

The audio voice asked where I was. Information started to come to me, but not in English, in another language. I heard the word *Altstat*. I knew that it was where I used to live, but everything was destroyed and overgrown. I was confused. I knew that I had had a family—a wife and five children—but everyone was gone. We had a very basic existence, like nomads. The audio voice asked, "What was your favorite thing to eat?" I answered, "Buttered potatoes."

The audio voice asked: "Are you married?" I could see my wife's face. I got the feeling that I wasn't a very good person. I could tell that I didn't love my wife, nor my children. I was a detached, coldhearted person. But that's what had helped me survive. I could just work and push through. I could feel the sense of work, work until exhaustion, and I saw visuals of trudging through the mud.

Words were coming in in a foreign language. The audio voice asked, "What is your name?" I heard something that sounded like "Ziguener." It was coming up for my family's name, too. I got to a point where I realized that I wasn't going to remember all these words, and so I got myself out of the meditation. I wrote down phonetically the words I remembered. I looked up the words. They were German. Only then did it occur to me that it was the Holocaust. The word *Ziguener* is the German word for "gypsy."

I pulled myself out of the meditation before I died, but my hunch is that I either killed myself or I died of starvation. My entire life was gone. I had no idea what had happened to my family.

My mom died two days later, so I didn't have time to analyze the PLR experience. Only much later did I find, in the Holocaust Encyclopedia on the website of the U.S. Holocaust Memorial Museum, in the section on tattoos,[33] that although most tattoos in Auschwitz were on the outside of the forearm, there was a period in early 1943 where the tattoos were on the inside of the forearm, like where mine is. I also found this: "Romani prisoners were given the letter Z ('*Zigeuner*' is German for 'Gypsy') in addition to the serial number." Then I realized that that's why I wanted a Z.

I never talked to anyone about my PLR. Then a few months ago, I was with my therapist, who is a licensed therapist with an MA, and we talked through my regression. It all lined up. It explained so many things in my life: my unhealthy cycles of work and deprivation of food, because work was how I survived and of course food was distributed only after work. In school when we studied the Holocaust, it was generally discussed that Jews were victims, but it was not mentioned that Roma,

33. United States Holocaust Memorial Museum, Holocaust Encyclopedia, "Tattoos and Numbers: The System of Identifying Prisoners at Auschwitz," https://encyclopedia.ushmm.org/content/en/article/tattoos-and-numbers-the-system-of-identifying-prisoners-at-auschwitz.

or gypsies, were also targets of Nazi genocide. After I graduated college, I decided to move to India and work with untouchables. *Zigeuner* literally means "untouchable."

I also realized that my friend Alex was my wife in that lifetime. I knew that I had not loved my wife. The dynamic that has gone on between Alex and me is that, although he is thirty years older than me, he is very devoted to me. Every week for years we would go to hear gypsy jazz together.

Why did I feel that getting a tattoo would protect me? Now I understand that if you were entering a concentration camp, getting tattooed is better than not getting tattooed because it means that you're going to be kept around. A tattoo meant survival.

Most people go for a PLR because they are plagued by physical or psychological problems that do not respond to traditional treatments. After years of practicing classical psychiatry, Dr. Brian Weiss, through his patient "Catherine," realized that "past-life therapy offered a rapid method of treating psychiatric symptoms, symptoms that had previously taken many months or years of costly therapy to alleviate.... Many [of my PLR subjects] were able to rid themselves of chronic lifelong symptoms, such as specific phobias, panic attacks, recurrent nightmares, unexplained fears, obesity, repeated destructive relationships, physical pain and illness, and so on."[34]

---

34. Brian L. Weiss, MD, *Through Time into Healing* (New York: Touchstone, 1992), p. 23.

Dr. Weiss holds that consciousness itself cures, that simply by becoming aware of the root of a problem in a past life, the problem itself disappears, although he does recommend post-PLR treatment with a certified psychotherapist in order to integrate the insights and information revealed. As he wrote: "They remember—names, dates, geography, details. And after they remember, like Catherine, they become cured."[35]

Other PLR therapists disagree. A PLR is like discovering a malevolent thief in your house at night. In order to banish the thief, is it sufficient to shine a flashlight on him, or must you also neutralize him with martial arts?

Efim Svirsky practices techniques akin to spiritual combat to neutralize past-life traumas. He helps his subjects enter into a state of deep relaxation, and then spends at least the first hour surrounding the subject with the healing light and love of God. When the subject actually sees or relives the past trauma, Svirsky guides the subject to eliminate the trauma with spiritual principles. After the patient reexperiences a traumatic death, Svirsky guides the victim to "go up with the soul" to the spiritual realms.

Svirsky regressed a Russian-born Jewish woman living in Israel. She went back to a lifetime in the Holocaust. She reported that she was going to the gas chambers. Feeling totally broken by the Nazis, she said, "They can do anything they want." She was totally depressed. As Svirsky describes the end of the session:

> You could see on her face that she was depressed. I took her through her death in the gas chambers. I told her, "Just go out of your body as it goes down

---

35. Ibid.

on the floor." You could see that as she went out of the body, her face changed, and there was a big smile. I asked her, "Why are you smiling?"

She replied, "Over there I had the total feeling that they won. Now I feel like they lost."[36]

A similar method is practiced by Svirsky's student and associate, Sasha Alexander Friedman, as described in the following case. Lea was born to a French Jewish family in 1985. From a young age, she had a phobia of trains. At nineteen, Lea married and moved to Israel. "I was constantly imagining where I would hide in case the Nazis would come," remembers Lea. "I would think of a hiding place, and then think it wasn't good enough and that they would find me. I was also afraid when my husband went to *kollel* (yeshivah for married men). I was afraid he wouldn't come back."

Lea also experienced physical ailments:

I went to many doctors, and nothing helped me until a doctor said it was psychological. Then I went to a woman who specialized in energy healing. When she reached the part of my body that hurt, I was in an alpha state, and I saw two images in my mind: one of a Nazi soldier and the other of Rabbi Elchonon Wasserman [a famous rabbi who lived in Baranovich, Poland]. I felt tremendous pain and started to cry. I understood I was there. I had no relief of my symptoms from this.

But then, two years later, I went to see Sasha Alexander, a healer who specializes in trauma. He

---

36. Interview with Efim Svirsky, December 13, 2017.

would lead me into a deep relaxation state and then would ask about my emotions, how I felt them, and which color they were. He had me imagine the light of God entering all of my body. I came to a black dot that was deeply rooted in my heart. He asked me to open it.

Then I remembered everything—that I was a seventeen-year-old girl who lived in Baranovich, and then I remembered being attacked by a Nazi soldier. I relived the trauma and cried a lot. Then Sasha helped me heal the pain. He told me to shine the light of God on the Nazi until he disappeared. Then he did other exercises. I had two sessions with him. After the first, the memory of the pain was tremendous, and I felt tremendously sad. After the second session, my symptoms disappeared immediately.

Carol Bowman, author of *Children's Past Lives,* also uses spiritual techniques to banish trauma for the three thousand subjects she has regressed in the last thirty years. A woman brought her seventeen-year-old daughter to Carol as a last-ditch effort after unsuccessfully seeing many psychotherapists. The girl had such serious separation anxiety that, although she had been accepted by a good college in another city, she refused to leave her family. This separation anxiety had plagued the girl throughout her life. She would not even go on school trips, faking illness to avoid them.

In her PLR, the girl saw herself as a mother in Germany during the Holocaust. She realized the war was going to get bad, so she decided to send her children away in order to protect them. She relived the wrenching scene of her young children going away. She was devastated. Had she made the right decision? She died in the war.

Carol then guided her into the afterlife state on the spiritual plane, and asked her to go back and see what happened to her children. She saw that they had survived the war and had ended up with decent lives. People had taken care of them. After the PLR, the girl's separation anxiety subsided and she was able to go away to college.[37]

Carol herself underwent her first PLR at the age of thirty-six. The winter before, for the third year in a row, she was battling pleurisy, asthma, pneumonia, and bronchial infections. In a spontaneous past-life recall, she saw herself as a man—a pianist—dying of tuberculosis. The following autumn, as Carol braced herself for another winter of pulmonary illness, a hypnotherapist named Norman Inge came to her town. In a PLR with Norman, Carol saw many scenes of her life as the pianist whom she had seen on his deathbed.

Then Norman suggested she go to another lifetime. She saw herself as a young girl of eleven or twelve playing a grand piano, an audition for acceptance to the Conservatory in Vienna. She then saw herself leaving Poland, and in a later scene she was a happy teenager in the Conservatory. Then her happiness turned to fear.

> "I see myself in a narrow apartment—I am in my mid- to late twenties, with two small children" [I told Norman]. "A grand piano fills one corner of the

---

37. Interview with Carol Bowman, March 18, 2018.

room. The door opens, and a young man wearing a beret walks in. I know he is my husband. He looks worried. The words 'It's too late' come to mind. I know that whatever he tells me has something to do with our being Jewish. My husband, who is a teacher at the university, speaks out against German policies. From the fear in his eyes, I know we're in trouble. I don't want to see what happens next."

Norman said, "Go on."

I curled up on the couch and held my knees; my stomach felt queasy, and I had to push out every word to describe what I saw next. "I see my two children, a little girl of about two and a boy about six. I'm holding their hands as we stand on a cobblestone street with many other people.... My husband is gone—I don't know where he is. They've taken him somewhere. The Germans are rounding us up. I'm scared for me and for my children."

I began to cry as I told Norman what I was seeing. Waves of sorrow swept through me. I shivered from cold as my plight got worse.[38]

Carol went on to describe a scene beside a train with soldiers and dogs. She was holding her daughter on her hip and her son with her free hand. She moaned and cried, but Norman urged her to go on.

"I'm in a camp. Everything is gray. I walk around numb. I don't know what's going on anymore. I

---

38. Carol Bowman, *Children's Past Lives*, pp. 42–43.

don't know what happened to my children or my husband. My family is gone, my music is gone. My spirit feels dead. I don't want to live anymore. Then I'm floating. I look down on an icy room with concrete walls. I see myself lying in a pile of twisted bodies. I've been gassed."[39]

After the PLR, Carol lay on the couch, drained from her emotions and her crying. "I now realized that I had been carrying the shadow of this woman's grief with me my whole life. What a relief to finally let it go! I felt lighter and clearer."[40]

Since childhood, Carol had a recurring, unsettling dream of a woman in a maroon coat, who was the same woman she saw in the PLR. After the PLR, she never had the dream again. Her yearly winter onslaughts of respiratory illnesses also never recurred.

Asked whether consciousness of a past trauma itself heals, Carol answers:

I don't think awareness alone can heal a traumatic past-life memory. The most effective way to heal a traumatic memory is to reexperience the trauma in the former persona, allow oneself to feel the emotions of the former experience, go through the death experience, and process it. I know from working with literally thousands of clients in the past thirty years that the best way to do this is with a skilled past-life therapist. It's difficult to do it on

---

39. Ibid., p. 43.
40. Ibid.

one's own, because most people are still stuck in the trauma and need assistance in going through the complete experience and understanding what thoughts, feelings, and physical sensations got locked into place at the time of death.

As I wrote in my book, the lung ailments I had for years healed after the catharsis during my PLR, because I felt safe enough working with a therapist to really look at what had happened in my former life, feel the sadness, fear, and anger, and release them after I "died" and left the body. That's when the real healing can occur. And I'm still getting insights into my present feelings and behaviors from that first regression I did thirty years ago.[41]

Often, people who go for PLR are surprised by what they discover. Rae Shagalov was born to a Jewish family in New Jersey in 1954. At the age of forty, Rae was planning her first trip to Israel, and she started having panic attacks where she experienced "feelings of claustrophobia like the world was closing in and feelings of suffocation." She went to a hypnotherapist to try to discover the source of these panic attacks.

Because Rae thought of her upcoming trip to Israel as a pilgrimage to the Western Wall, the last remaining vestige of the Holy Temple that was destroyed two thousand years ago, she expected that her PLR would take her to a traumatic

---

41. Carol Bowman, email to the author, March 14, 2018.

death associated with the Temple's destruction. Instead, recalls Rae, "in the hypnosis I was a young teenage girl who jumped alive into a mass grave, where people were being shot and falling in. I was trying to hide, but I suffocated under them."

Sometimes in a PLR a person discovers a previous identity that is utterly alien to her, like a girl growing up in a Boston Brahmin family and discovering as an adult that she was adopted, and her biological mother was an Albanian immigrant who just before she was born got off a boat very different from the *Mayflower*. Such is the case of Kathy Boyer, who was born into a Roman Catholic family in Malone, New York, in 1960. As an adult, she experimented with other Christian denominations. Although Kathy had a heightened sensitivity to Holocaust video footage and movies, she had no Holocaust-related dreams nor phobias.

Growing up, Kathy did not believe in reincarnation, but at the age of fifty-seven, she read some literature that alluded to it. Finding herself on vacation in Virginia Beach, near the Edgar Cayce A.R.E. (Association for Research and Enlightenment) Center, Kathy decided to go there for a PLR. "It led me to a lifetime as a Jewish man named Ephraim, during the Holocaust, who was killed in the gas chambers. This is not what I was expecting to see during a regression, and it caught me pretty much off guard."

As Kathy describes the PLR: "The first thing I saw was a lot of concrete buildings. My mind said, 'Germany.'" The hypnotherapist asked Kathy what she looked like. "I was taken aback, because I wasn't prepared to see myself as a man, but I saw a clear face of a young man with a hat on that was 1940s era." Then the therapist asked her what her name was. The Hebrew name *Ephraim* popped into her mind.

> She asked me what I did for a living, and I saw myself near some sort of printing machine. I perceived that I was working for a newspaper, and that I was a newspaper editor. She asked me to go to a "happy occasion" during that time, and my mind went to a Jewish wedding. I saw the woman I was married to. She had long black hair and a long, thin face and a small, thin frame. The Jewish wedding had a lot of dancing.
>
> Then she asked me to go to a sad time, and I went to a place where I was alone. I seemed to be somewhat "inside my mind at that time," realizing that I was in a prison/gas chamber setting, although I didn't see anyone or anything else around me, only that I was alone and I was going to die. I missed my "wife" from that incarnation, and felt like life was taken from me too soon. Then she asked me to transition to when I was leaving my body, to transition to the other side, and who was there to greet me. There was a group of people, and I didn't think to see if I recognized anyone....
>
> The information I did receive has helped me understand and explain some things from this lifetime. In particular, I have always had a *compulsion* to edit and correct anything I see written down anywhere—even letters that people write to me! I'm

constantly correcting (at least in my mind) grammar, spelling, punctuation, wording, etc.

The other thing is that during my life, I have a *total aversion* to watching anything related to the Holocaust. It bothers me so badly. Going back to high school, when they showed original footage from World War II, it was awful, and deeply saddened me. I went to see the movie *Sophie's Choice* when I was in college, not realizing what the subject matter was, and it was a dreadful experience. That was the last thing I really ever watched on the Holocaust.

Trudi Goodman also discovered an unlikely previous identity during a PLR. Trudi was born to a Jewish family in Boston in 1954. As related in chapter 6, as a tour guide in Boston, she had a hatred of hearing people speak German.

In her PLR, Trudi saw herself not as a Jew, but as an Italian soldier in Yugoslavia, assigned to fight with the Nazis.

I was part of shooting there. I shot people. I had tremendous guilt about it. Later on, in a town in Italy that I grew up in, I saw that I tried to stop Jews from being killed. I saw a man I had known my whole life who was a Jew shot in front of me. I was shot by the Germans for trying to help Jews and others escape from that roundup. As I was dying, I made a conscious decision that I wanted to come back as a Jew in my next life, in order to redeem my soul.[42]

---

42. A non-Jewish soul cannot become a Jewish soul except through conversion

In his research, Dr. Brian Weiss connected physical symptoms in this lifetime in hundreds of cases with a violent death in a previous lifetime. For example, Elaine, a respected psychologist, suffered intermittent, excruciating pains in her neck, shoulders, and upper back. In a PLR, she saw herself as a soldier of a defeated army, his hands tied, being lanced in his upper back. For a few days after the PLR, she was in agony, but then her back pain totally disappeared. In another PLR, Elaine saw herself in medieval France, being accused of a crime and hanged. After this PLR, her chronic neck pain disappeared.[43]

This book tells of multiple cases of people who purportedly died in the gas chambers or were suffocated in the killing pits under other bodies who in this lifetime suffer from respiratory problems. Another example of physical symptoms in this lifetime connected to a violent death in World War II is the case of Breindy, born to a Jewish family in Brooklyn in 1948. Breindy suffers from irritable bowel syndrome and migraines. In a PLR, she was surprised to see herself as a German soldier. As a boy, he had joined the Hitler Youth, then later worked in Buchenwald as a guard. He was transferred to the Russian front, where he was killed. In the PLR, Breindy saw herself as that German soldier in a long gray coat. He was stabbed in the stomach and shot in the head, the locations of her physical maladies in this lifetime.[44]

---

according to halachah. My hypothesis in Trudi's case is that she was a Jewish soul who was born as an Italian non-Jew who became a soldier in World War II. That may explain why he sacrificed his life by trying to save Jews. In her next lifetime, her soul returned as a Jew in Boston.

43. Weiss, *Through Time into Healing*, p. 52.

44. Perhaps Breindy, too, was a Jewish soul born into a non-Jewish body in her

Fally Klein and Morris Srour are PLR hypnotherapists and also Orthodox Jews. Several years ago, they walked into a training session, and the hypnotized subject said to them: "You're Jews. You need to help me."

The woman, a non-Jew, had grown up in Africa and at that point lived in Greece, far from anyone Jewish. She used to wake up with words on her lips that she didn't understand. She wrote them down phonetically. She had two words she kept repeating: "*tzavaat chayim*" and "*orlah.*"

During her PLR, she started speaking a language that Fally and Morris recognized as Hebrew. She went back to a chaotic scene of bombing and helicopters. She was a man. His wife was packing to leave. "I never said goodbye to her," the subject lamented.

Fally took her back to early childhood in that lifetime. The man had grown up in a wealthy Jewish family in Romania. Fally asked her to write down her name. Strangely, the subject started writing from right to left. The first letter was a circle and a line, which Fally knew was the Hebrew letter *alef.* Asked to read the name, the subject said, "Aviram." She described her life as a boy growing up in a family where they cared much about being respected.

Fally asked her to go forward to a happy time. The subject saw her own wedding in the family home. The subject started singing "*Od Yishama,*" the traditional Jewish wedding song. Fally then asked her to describe the wedding ring given to the bride. Orthodox Jews generally use a plain, unadorned gold band. The subject said that there were letters on the inside of

previous lifetime.

the band, and proceeded to describe letters that Fally recognized as Hebrew.

Next, Fally asked her to go to the end of her life. She saw herself dying as an old man, having survived the Holocaust. "I need you to take something," she said to Fally. Fally stuck out her hand to receive the invisible object and asked, "What's this?"

"It's my *tzavaat chayim*." Fally understood these Hebrew words, which mean "last will and testament." The subject went on: "It tells my story. You need to get this to my nephews." She named three Jewish names. "They need to know. They need to know what happened to us."

At that point Fally knew it was time to help this soul be free to move on. As Fally explains, "Often souls that feel they have unfinished business linger in this realm until they are reassured it's safe to move on. I stepped into the session to give the lingering soul the reassurance it needed to finally stop visiting the client in her dreams and move on."

She announced, "My name is Fally Klein. The year is 2015. The world did not forget. The world knows what happened."

As Fally described what transpired next: "*Swish!* He was out of the body. He was excited. He saw his wife. He said, 'I love her so much.'"

Fally asked him, "Why have you been coming in dreams with the word *orlah*?" Fally knew that "*orlah*" means the foreskin that is removed from a Jewish baby at the time of circumcision.

The subject, still under hypnosis, replied, "Because I wanted you to know who I am. *Orlah*. It makes me a Jewish man." Fally played dumb. The subject continued, "I cannot talk about this. You know how this makes me a Jewish man. But it's not appropriate to talk about. There are women in this room. This is not something we talk about in front of women."

A week later, the subject sent Fally a message from Greece. She had woken up with the word *Yehud* on her lips. *Yehud* means Jew.

Weighing in on the question whether consciousness alone heals, Fally Klein gives a robust no. She declares: "There's no such thing as just go and watch the movie. This is soul work. You're working with soul memories, and you must do the work: learning, forgiving, releasing trauma. When facilitating a PLR, a skilled hypnotherapist will ask the client questions such as, 'What were your accomplishments? Any unfinished business? Did you need to say goodbye? Do you have any regrets? Do you need to do any work before leaving that state? Why would you choose that life?'"[45]

From that perspective, a PLR is less like watching a movie and more like being the film critic who analyzes every nuance of plot and action, convinced that every story has a lesson hidden within it. This world has no spectators, only virtuoso actors.

Spontaneous past-life recall is similar to memories of this lifetime. Just as you may remember your cousin's birthday party, with the balloons and the cake, when you were eight

---

45. Interview with Fally Klein, December 3, 2017.

years old and reexperience the embarrassment you felt when someone made fun of you, so you may remember the details of a scene in a previous lifetime and reexperience the accompanying emotions. Spontaneous past-life recall is usually triggered by a similar situation or place.

In her book *Children's Past Lives*, Carol Bowman relates the experience of three-year-old Lauren Green, who lived in rural Illinois. Her mother, Karen, was driving Lauren home from the dentist, where the child had had six silver crowns put on her back teeth. Suddenly Lauren said, "I don't like having silver teeth, because remember when we died together and those bad guys took our silver teeth?" As Karen described her own reaction:

> When she said that, my heart began pounding wildly and my body began to shake. I pulled to the side of the road for a minute, so I wouldn't have an accident. Since we are Jewish, I knew immediately that she was talking about the Holocaust. [The Nazis extracted the gold and silver out of the mouths of many of their victims.] I knew that I had not misunderstood her words; I knew that she was not playing a game. I honestly didn't think it could have been anything else. I could feel the truth of what she was saying....
>
> The chances that Lauren could have known this detail are absolutely zero. Even my ten-year-old, who now knows what the Holocaust is, would not know such a detail as having teeth taken out of your mouth. They certainly haven't watched anything on TV about this; I haven't read anything to them

about the Holocaust. I would never want to scare
them about such things.[46]

Such spontaneous remarks by young children form the
basis of Dr. Ian Stevenson's copious research on reincarnation. Like Karen Green, virtually all the mothers in cases
investigated by Stevenson took their children's inexplicable
statements seriously, which encouraged the children to elab-
orate. Stevenson speculates that where parents dismiss their
children's past-life descriptions as ridiculous, the children
are unlikely to speak about them again. This explains why
Stevenson found thousands of children to research in India,
Sri Lanka, and Burma, where reincarnation is accepted and
the parents took serious note of their children's statements
that pointed to a past life. His final book, *European Cases of the
Reincarnation Type*, reports on a mere 32 cases, selected from
250 European cases that came to his attention, most of which
he did not feel met his rigorous research criteria.

The case of Teuvo Koivisto, born in Helsinki, Finland, in
1971 to a Lutheran family, was researched by Stevenson and
his assistant Rita Castren, both of whom interviewed Teuvo's
mother Lusa in Helsinki.

Lusa at the age of sixteen had an experience of spontaneously remembering a previous life in France at the time
of the French Revolution. As Professor Stevenson remarks,
"These experiences prepared Lusa to listen attentively when
Teuvo spoke about a previous life."[47]

---

46. Carol Bowman, *Children's Past Lives: How Past Life Memories Affect Your Child*
(New York: Bantam Books, 1997), p. 185.

47. Ian Stevenson, MD, *European Cases of the Reincarnation Type* (Jefferson, North

Teuvo started speaking fluently at the age of three. One morning he woke up and surprised his mother Lusa by telling her that he had been alive before. Teuvo was "extremely frightened" and "terrified" as he described to his mother his memories:

> He referred to "the big furnace." He gave some details about the furnace. He mentioned that the people were piled higgledy-piggledy in layers in the furnace. Some were lying on top of others. He said that he had been taken to the "bathroom." Personal objects were removed from the people in the bathroom, such as their eyeglasses and their golden teeth. Then the people were undressed and put into the furnace. Gas came pouring out of some place in the walls. He could not breathe. Teuvo said that he "knew" that he was going to be put in the furnace, but he did not say that he had actually been put in the furnace. He said that he came to his mother after seeing the others being put there. Teuvo also described an "oven" with children in it.
>
> After Teuvo had made these statements, he added: "Then I came to you. I was given here. Are you happy, Mummy, that I came to you?"[48]

In an interview with Professor Stevenson's research assistant Rita Castren in 1976, Lusa testified that her son continued to speak about such memories for about half a

---

Carolina: McFarland & Co., 2001), p. 164.

48. Ibid., p. 165.

year, always when he awoke in the morning. With the onset of these memories, Teuvo developed difficulty in breathing, where it seemed painful for him to breathe. These attacks, which each lasted ten to fifteen minutes, occurred sometimes twice a week, and sometimes at an interval of three months. Lusa took Teuvo to a physician, who ascertained that he did not have asthma. The periodic breathing difficulty persisted at least until Teuvo was seven years old.

Professor Stevenson assiduously investigated the possibility that his research subjects might have acquired their information of distant times and places from "normal sources," such as television or hearing family members speak about the subject.

> Lusa declared firmly that Teuvo could not have acquired the information he had about German concentration camps normally. He was rarely allowed to watch television and never any program showing violence. His parents and his older brothers never discussed such matters as concentration camps and gas chambers in the presence of Teuvo.[49]

Adults also experience spontaneous past-life recall. Glenn J. Hill was born to a Methodist family in Sacramento, California, in 1953. Although his family ostensibly had no Jewish connections, by fourth grade Glenn was reading everything he could find about the Holocaust. He studied German

---

49. Ibid., p. 166.

in high school and did his class paper on German art under the Nazis.

On September 21, 1999, near sunset that day, at the age of forty-six, Glenn died for five minutes from anaphylactic shock. He had walked into the ER with only a 0.5 blood oxygen level, while normal is 75–100. He spent the next nineteen hours on life support. Unknown to Glenn, this was the start of Yom Kippur, the day in the Jewish calendar when God decides who shall live and who shall die. Glenn experienced a classic near-death episode.

Then, two weeks later, Glenn had a spontaneous PLR.

In the past life I have recalled, my wife and I were together as a couple, with her not being Jewish, and me being so, but being assimilated, not traditionally Jewish. I was Italian, spiritually progressive, an avant-garde artist. We were very wealthy, living on the coast near Genoa, very longtime family in the area. My name was Alberto Carnegie (I'm not sure of the last name spelling, but it sounds like this). Men in black shirts broke into our home, slashed my paintings and destroyed my art studio. I was beaten, taken out and shot with rifle fire to my chest, and then a pistol shot to the head, in front of my wife and our two little girls, who were screaming in terror. Our two little girls were taken away to a camp. My wife was left alone, as she was not Jewish. She later killed herself in despair, jumping off the cliff into the sea.

I have recalled that our house, a villa really, was on the edge of a cliff overlooking the sea, outside of Genoa, Italy, to the east, near Portofino. The first flash of memory was followed by more scenes and information over a period of time, including a scene of riding with my family in a beautiful luxurious open car near the sea.

Two years later, in 2001, Glenn entered a synagogue for the first time. His wife was taking a course in helping terminally ill people through the dying process, and the course involved studying different religions. They decided that it would be an educational experience to go to Rosh HaShanah services.

When I came to the door of the synagogue, I was suddenly stopped halfway in and halfway out by a deep, visceral terror, a strong fear that my life would be in danger if I crossed through that doorway. I think I was apparently deeply afraid at the time to be identified as a Jew, as a memory from my past-life experiences. But I did step through the door.

Several years later, Glenn discovered that his matrilineal line traced back to Jewish ancestors who had fled Portugal, arriving in Virginia in the early 1700s. With that, Glenn started to identify as a Jew and to affiliate with the Jewish Renewal movement, studying Judaism under Reb Zalman Schachter-Shalomi. One Yom Kippur he was in the synagogue when, for the first time in his life, he was handed the Torah scroll to hold.

When I took the Torah, I suddenly felt this over-whelming grief, which in a few minutes had me sobbing. I realized that this grief came from having chosen not to have ever held the Torah in a past life. I was aware that in at least one past lifetime (the Italian one), I had rejected the Jewish religion as "out of date." I had died in that lifetime because I was Jewish, even though I was not religious.

I think the lesson in that life was that I did not take seriously that the Fascists in Italy were a threat to me, an assimilated Jew.

The most important thing, I believe, is to learn the lesson that each of us did not learn in our last lifetime. It is for that purpose that we have come back.

Beverly, born to a Jewish family in New York in 1960, experienced a spontaneous past-life recall at the age of thirty-one. A family therapist and a follower of the Lubavitcher Rebbe, Beverly had always felt pain in her chest. She went to many cardiologists, who ascertained that she had no heart problems. When she was expecting her fourth child, Beverly went to the home of a shiatsu practitioner for a massage. The woman's two-year-old son was playing with toy soldiers on the floor nearby.

I was awake, and very relaxed. She started to work on my chest. Suddenly, I felt this terror, like I fell into a three-dimensional black hole. The little boy said, "Soldier! Soldier!" I had a horrific terror, like I've never experienced in my life, and I saw a vision of a little girl (maybe eight years old) on her knees, with her hand reaching up. I saw black boots, and that second I was shot in the chest, and I died.

I started screaming like I've never screamed in my life. The practitioner held me for about two hours. I didn't know if I'd ever be normal again, because I felt I had witnessed my own murder. Then, as I was lying there, a vision of the Lubavitcher Rebbe came into my head, and he said, "You will be okay." He reassured me three times.

When I calmed down, after two hours, the practitioner looked at me and said, "You were there, and I was also there, in Holland. I was a non-Jew who saved Jews."

That was it. I never had anything like it before or since. For three days after that experience, I was completely calm and peaceful, like life took on a different sensation, one of acceptance. I had no need for anything, like more money or more accomplishments. There was a deep, deep peace, like the deepest trust in God, that everything was from Him.

While some PLRs reveal surprising identities, in most cases a person intuits who she may have been in a past lifetime, and the PLR only confirms it. Ludmila Duhot was born into a Christian Orthodox family in Moldova in 1985. As a child, she had recurring dreams of being in a train stuffed with people. Although she was growing up in a Christian family that never discussed the Holocaust, young Ludmila was obsessed with the subject. "I had to watch all the documentaries and movies, and I was crying and crying."

When Ludmila was seventeen, she became an exchange student in Germany. During her first week there, she went with a group of other students to visit a concentration camp. "I immediately knew," remembers Ludmila, "that I am personally connected to this story."

During a PLR years later, Ludmila saw herself as a young Jewish girl who was adopted by a German family. The Nazis discovered that she had Jewish roots, took her away, and sent her to a concentration camp.

An even more dramatic instance of the subjective element in identifying a past life is the case of Michel Savanes. When Michel experienced an intense emotional and physical reaction to hearing a poem, accompanied by a sense of recognition, he was led on a surprising journey to understand his reaction.

Michel, born into a Jewish family in Casablanca, Morocco, in 1946, experienced a self-induced PLR through a meditative technique. At the age of forty-six, while working as a radio operator in the Israeli merchant marine, Michel decided to utilize a process of entering into an alpha state in order to "relive" past traumatic experiences that may have been affecting him in the present. He saw himself as a boy in what was evidently the Holocaust. In one scene, he was crouched in what seemed like a hideout, and was writing with great concentration in a notebook.

I was very intrigued by this, as I wondered whatever happened to that notebook.

A couple years later, on the eve of Israel's Holocaust Day of 1994, I was home and watching on television the live broadcast of the ceremony from Yad Vashem. At some point the MC was reading out a poem, and as I heard the words of that poem, I started experiencing strange phenomena, feeling emotional and confused, thinking to myself, *I know this poem, but from where?* and *This is something that I wrote,* then brushing off the idea as weird. But the feeling kept growing stronger. I was having knots in my stomach. I felt transported. Then the reading of the poem ended, and the MC said, "This poem was written by a young Jewish boy from Poland who could have grown to become a famous poet or writer, but he died at age fifteen in Auschwitz."

At this point I remembered that notebook in which I had seen myself writing, and I instantly made the connection. I knew that this poem was taken from my notebook. I felt relief, realizing that the notebook I had seen in my past-life recall wasn't lost and was in existence somewhere.

For the next six years, Michel did nothing to follow up on his past-life recall as the boy in hiding writing in the notebook. Then, one day in the year 2000, in timing that proved to be serendipitous and fateful, he decided to go to Yad Vashem and try to find the notebook.

I had no idea what was going to ensue. First, I visited the museum and saw my notebook (the original) as an exhibit within a glass enclosure. Then I went down to the archives to try and obtain more information about how it was recovered and got to Yad Vashem. This culminated in my being shown a hardcover book published by Yad Vashem, entitled in Hebrew *Mishel Atzmi* [*From Myself*] by Abramek Koplowicz. Since my name in this lifetime is Michel [pronounced "Mishel"], this was unreal. I had to sit down and suppress an emotional outburst.

I didn't leave Yad Vashem without buying myself a copy of that book. It contains eight poems, two sketches, and a drawing, all by Abramek. It has an introduction written by Eliezer Greenfelt, Abramek's half-brother, who was born to Abramek's widowed father when he remarried after the war.

I was so carried away by all this that once I got home I made a point of obtaining this man's phone number and calling him. And I could not have imagined the exact timing of what was awaiting me. I introduced myself as someone who found Abramek's book and was deeply touched by it and wanted to know more about him. His response was, "Come to the Holon theater this evening at eight o'clock. We're having a special memorial event for Abramek."

I went! What an experience.... Sitting there in a packed room, and attending this memorial for "me." I ended up meeting with this man and his whole family, and we've become friends. And in the process, I found out about the extensive work that's been done in making Abramek's story and poems known, translated to various languages, and much more. The city of Lodz in Poland has a street named after Abramek Koplowicz, and he has been included among the national poets of Poland.

As you can tell, this series of events seems surreal, almost spooky. But to me this is truly real, and it boils down to my "finding" the notebook in my recall process first, and then after seeking to find out what had happened to it, actually finding the notebook in real life.

CHAPTER 8

EMERGENCY LANDINGS: JEWISH SOULS IN CHRISTIAN BODIES

MIRELLE JANE MILLAR, GROWING UP in a small town in the cane-farming country of North Queensland, Australia, did not know a single Jew. Born in Whangārei, New Zealand, in 1980 to Pentecostal Christian parents who were both pastors, the only thing Mirelle knew about Judaism was that the Christian savior was born Jewish. She learned nothing about the Holocaust in school.

As a child of four or five, Mirelle would say peculiar things, such as, "I don't eat ham," and "I don't eat bacon," and "Saturday is the day of rest, not Sunday." Her parents, who led a small church, indulged their daughter. She never had to eat the foods of which she disproved. The child had a single phobia: German shepherd dogs.

At the age of nine, Mirelle was in a video store with her mother and older brothers. Normally she would pick Mary Poppins, but that day she noticed a video called *Escape from Sobibor*. She wanted to get it. Her brothers told her that it wasn't for children, but Mirelle insisted she must watch it. Her mom, unaware of the horrific content of the television movie portraying the death camp where two hundred and fifty thousand people were exterminated, was curious, and rented the movie.

Sitting in their living room that night watching the video, nine-year-old Mirelle announced, "I know this story." Her mother assured her that she didn't, but young Mirelle was adamant that she recognized everything. In the scene where a German shepherd attacks a woman, Mirelle cried out, "That's why I hate German shepherds!" In the last scene of the film, where most of the prisoners are killed during their desperate escape, Mirelle began to cry.

"I had this sense," she remembered three decades later, "that I need to find the people who survived. I knew they were my people."

For Mirelle, watching *Escape from Sobibor* was like opening a door to a dark tunnel. She started having recurring nightmares about the Holocaust that plagued her for the rest of her childhood and throughout her teenage years. She became obsessed with Jews (of whom she still had not met a single one) and with Israel. While none of her friends had even heard of the Holocaust, she voraciously read Holocaust books and saw films.

At the age of seventeen, she left school and went to spend a year in Israel. Her parents meanwhile moved back to New Zealand. When the time came to leave Israel and return to New Zealand to start university, Mirelle was heartbroken. Eventually, she converted to Judaism.

> I went through my conversion a few years ago, after years of trying to search for why I was so connected to Jewish culture, Judaism, the Holocaust, and Israel. I came to the conclusion that I have a Jewish soul and reincarnated into a non-Jewish family, and that my past life most likely had been in the Holocaust. As a child I knew things and had memories of things that were not told to me. During my interview with the rabbis prior to my conversion, they acknowledged my belief that I had a Jewish soul. Following conversion, it has been like my soul is at peace.

Reincarnation assumes the existence of a spiritual entity, the soul, that continues to exist after the death of the physical body, and can enter a new body later in time. Just as horticulturalists know the difference between the twenty-eight thousand species of orchids, Kabbalists, who are experts in souls, know the difference between different "species" of souls. One of those "species" is a Jewish soul. While a Jewish person is someone born to a Jewish mother or who has undergone halachic conversion, a Jewish soul, according to Rav Yitzchak Luria, the great sixteenth-century Kabbalist known as the Arizal, can be born in a non-Jewish body in order to affect a rectification or learn a particular lesson. Nevertheless, most Jewish souls are born to Jewish mothers.

The Holocaust, however, created an emergency situation. According to the revered Klausenberger Rebbe, Rav Yekusiel Yehuda Halberstam, who himself was a Holocaust survivor and lost his wife and eleven children, after the Holocaust millions of souls had to come back, but there weren't enough Jewish mothers to receive them. So they went to non-Jewish mothers.[50]

This is the phenomenon described by Daniel O., who was born into a Protestant family in St. Petersburg, Florida. He rejected Christianity at a very early age, and converted to Judaism at the age of thirty-one.

> I too am one of the returned. I was born in 1954 to a non-Jewish family. It's a long story, but the short version is that I was always plagued by nightmares of fighting, sometimes solo combat, sometimes terrible battles. In meditation I have become convinced that my soul has returned from a previous incarnation as a nonobservant Jewish partisan killed during World War II. I believe there simply were not enough Jewish babies for us all to return in, so I came back as a gentile, and recognized myself as a Jew.
>
> After doing a dream workshop with a Jewish Renewal rabbi about seventeen years ago, where I mentioned the nightmares, he suggested wearing

---

50. Quoted by one of my interviewees, who worked with the Klausenberger Rebbe to establish Laniado Hospital in Netanya.

a *kippah* constantly. I have since worn a yarmulke consistently, and the bad dreams have never returned.

Belinda was born in Hobart, Tasmania, in 1957 to a Christian family who had become avowed atheists and practiced no religion. She knew no Jews and knew nothing about the Holocaust. From the age of eight, she had dreams of being imprisoned in a camp and fearing for her life. "The men had uniforms and boots on," she recalls. "In the dream I was running. It was not until years later when I saw pictures of the Holocaust that I recognized these men as Nazis."

Belinda was sent to a private girls' school that taught a course in world religions. She was thirteen when, as part of the course, the teacher took the class to a defunct synagogue in Hobart. As soon as Belinda entered the synagogue, she started crying. When it was time to leave, she did not want to go. The caretaker was a Holocaust survivor. "I didn't want to leave his presence. It was as if I had known him all my life. He was the first Jew I ever met."

After that experience, Belinda "devoured everything I could lay my hands on in regard to the Shoah, Judaism, and Zionism." At the age of twenty-one, she converted to Judaism.

A Jewish soul in a non-Jewish body will feel uncomfortable in its non-Jewish identity, like a person wearing a parka in Tahiti. The soul will feel an inexplicable pull toward Judaism, and in many cases will end up converting. Judaism is a religion that does not missionize and, in fact, discourages conversion. A rabbi is obligated by Jewish law to turn away a prospective convert three times. Those who persevere in wanting to convert must study Judaism for at least a year and usually much longer. Nevertheless, in this post-Holocaust era, many determined people continue to convert to Judaism.

The story of Dana Wespiser, born to a Catholic family in San Jose, California, in 1962, illustrates the discomfort of a Jewish soul in a non-Jewish family. Dana had an "overwhelming horror" of the church building and of the people attending mass.

> From the earliest age I can remember, I had absolute panic attacks at the thought of having to "go to church." I would intentionally lose my white church shoes in order not to go, because one can't enter that place without shoes, now, can they? Clever. We were never spoiled, so I wasn't immediately bought another pair of shoes, but it did cause quite a ruckus.
>
> My other main ploy to get out of the absolute terror I felt upon having to go to church was to hide, anywhere and everywhere—closets, outside, up the street. I'd often hide behind the big, wooden stereo console, or in the drapes. I would kick, scream, *anything* not to go to church. My parents were not abusive, so they would try to persuade me, or give up occasionally and insist on leaving me with my friend next door with the deal I go with her family later (which rarely happened).

In Sunday school, which Dana was forced to attend from first grade, she was a rebellious student. She once asked the nun, "How can God be God and yet a person? It doesn't make sense." The nun called Dana "a Jew," and threw her out of class.

When little Dana came home, she asked her mother, "Are we Jewish?"

Her mother snapped, "No! Don't ever ask that again."

At some point in her adolescence, Dana found a very old book belonging to her mother, *A Treasury of Jewish Folklore*. It contained the musical notation for Shema and another Jewish liturgical prayer.

> It mesmerized me. I'd play it over and over again on my flute and vowed to become a Jew (again). I felt I had always been one, just the body wasn't kosher, so to speak. I underwent an Orthodox conversion in 2003, in Baltimore, and made aliyah in 2007.
>
> I believe very much that I was taken away from my Jewish family and raised during the Holocaust with non-Jews, unwillingly, and in this incarnation I converted back into *am Yisrael*, as my soul seems not at all new, but very old and complex. Even my own family always would joke that I wasn't really one of them, that I was different.... I always felt that my family was, plainly, the wrong one.

A similar feeling of being out of place besieged Marcella Roberts, who was born in 1963 in Rochester, New York, to a Catholic family with German roots that proudly traced its history in America to the 1690s. From an early age, Marcella had a recurring dream where she was always trying to hide from soldiers. "In my dream," she recalls, "sometimes I'm hiding in a house, sometimes outside in the freezing cold, and sometimes trying to hide something from someone (like my identity)."

> From a very young age, I always felt different. Although I grew up surrounded by Christians, I never took to the Christian narrative. It wasn't until graduate school that my clinical director said that with all of my values and not believing in their god that I must be Jewish. I disclosed to her that I have always felt that. This catapulted me into my Jewish learning and conversion.

Another oft-mentioned phenomenon among many of my Christian-born survey respondents is the intuitive feeling from a young age of already being Jewish. As Georgene Powell, who was born to a Christian family in Phoenix, Arizona, in 1946 (and whose Holocaust dreams appear in chapter 3), put it: "I was born a Christian, but felt Jewish since I was a child. I finally, finally made my Jewish soul legal by converting in 2001, when I developed the self-confidence to do so."

Another example of such "becoming who you are" is a woman born in the United Kingdom in 1965 to a family that belongs to the Church of England. Obsessed with the Holocaust since the age of five, she converted to Judaism as an adult. She writes, "Since converting I am still a 'lone Jew.' My family finds it strange, but at last I feel myself. I am a professional with master's degrees and have always felt, before my conversion, like a misfit. Now I am just myself as I was meant to be."

This triple pattern, of childhood Holocaust dreams, not fitting into their Christian family, and feeling intuitively that they are Jewish, recurred in many of my survey respondents. Capucine Frandeen was born to a Christian family in Oregon in 1952. Her dream of swinging above a pit of fire and having to choose two people to save, and finally dropping down into the pit, appears in chapter 3. She had this dream almost every night from the age of three until she was seven or eight.

> I decided I was Jewish from a young age, but never declared I was until my mother died when I was twelve. At her funeral I said to myself, "Today I'm a Jew," but I didn't know a single Jew.
>
> After that, I told everyone who asked what religion I was that I was Jewish. I felt it very strongly and wore a star of David. I didn't know any Jews or have any knowledge about anything other than Yom Kippur, Rosh HaShanah, Pesach, Chanukah, and kashrut (on a very low level). All my knowledge was gleaned from the Encyclopedia Britannica. I couldn't keep kosher exactly because I was living with my family, so I told them that I was vegetarian.
>
> We moved overseas. In my teens, my Jewish friends made fun of me that I kept kosher and that I had the biggest Holocaust library of anyone they knew.
>
> When I graduated from TAIS (Taipei American International School), I went to California and got

> a job and went to night classes at San Mateo City College, with the intention of saving money and making my way to Israel. For my telecom class in college, I made a very short documentary on children of Holocaust survivors. I especially chose Jewish students for my crew, thinking they would be supportive of my project. I was shocked to find that they were far less interested than I.
>
> At the age of twenty, I converted to Judaism.

The sense of familiarity with Jews and Judaism by people never exposed to either may be a telltale sign of a Jewish soul. Dolly Smith was born in Sioux City, Iowa, to an Episcopalian family that never discussed the Holocaust. Yet Dolly had Holocaust-related dreams starting in the third grade until she was a teenager. In her nightmares, she was chased by dogs, and also had a fear of being burned.[51]

One day when she was eleven years old, Dolly had what would be described as a flashback. On a snowy day, she was playing outside with her friends when she suddenly felt like she was on fire. She smelled smoke. Confused and scared, she ran inside to her grandmother.

The only two Jews Dolly knew in Sioux City were her pediatrician, Dr. Levy, and her classmate Golda. One day in fifth grade, Golda invited Dolly to her house to play after school. "The moment I walked in," remembers Dolly, "I felt like I was

---

51. Fear of being burned could be connected to a traumatic death not in the Holocaust, such as being burned at the stake during the Inquisition. However, such deaths would not be connected to being chased by dogs, which the Nazis used to sniff out Jews in hiding.

home. That point in time opened a thirst in me for anything Jewish." Eventually Dolly converted to Judaism.

Some Holocaust souls pay a high price for their decision to convert to Judaism. Margaret Ann Rice was born in Mt. Clemens, Michigan, in 1951. Her birth mother surrendered her for adoption a few days after birth. Her adopted parents, Doris and Bill, as well as Doris's parents, Tom and Helen, were all devoted churchgoers, members of the Episcopalian Church. Margaret, raised as an only child, was the apple of her family's eye. She sang in church and, with her family, attended church at least twice a week, for services and various activities. She was baptized, and confirmed at the age of fourteen.

Around that time, she began having a recurring dream. She saw herself as a twelve-year-old boy, standing outdoors, freezing, in some sort of camp.

> The sounds are terrifying. The smell is terrifying. I look at the trees and know I am going to die that day. People are speaking German. I understand the language easily. This dream recurs even until today.
>
> I have claustrophobia when in enclosed rooms made of wood. As soon as I went to Dachau at age thirty-four, I recognized the wooden rooms as the barracks. I recognized the layout of the camp. I recognized the trees, although they are much taller

now. I recognized the spot where I was standing when I thought to myself, *I am going to die today.*

In preparation for confirmation at the age of fourteen, Margaret began reading the works of Paul Tillich, Franz Rosenzweig, Dietrich Bonhoeffer, Thomas Merton, and Martin Buber. Buber's philosophy deeply affected her, as she wrote:

> After reading *I and Thou*, the concept of the Trinity no longer resonated with me. The idea of requiring a conduit in order to have a legitimate encounter with the Divine made no sense to me. I thought about this for quite a while (about a year) and then stopped going to church entirely.
>
> My (adopted) parents completely freaked out. They had the priest talk to me several times. My grandparents Tom and Helen actually stopped speaking to me, unless it was absolutely necessary. I had been quite close to Tom, my grandfather. He taught me how to read music, how to perform in public (I sing), and how to draw. He also taught me to ice skate and to swim and to row. The decision to stop going to church pretty much ended the relationship. That was the most painful loss....
>
> I determined while I was still in high school that I would need to convert to Judaism—but at that point, I had absolutely no idea how or when or under what circumstances my conversion would occur. I just kept reading and thinking during my high school years. I didn't know a single Jew until I

was eighteen, but I was so obsessed with Judaism that my closest friends would tease me about it. (Like giving me a paperback entitled *1000 Jewish Jokes* as a birthday gift.)

When I left home to attend college, I immediately signed up for classes in Jewish thought at the campus Hillel. I had a wonderful rabbi as an instructor there for about five years. I was part of a *havarah* (an informal community for study and prayer) during law school. The final semester in law school (spring 1979), I realized that I felt ready, that I knew enough, and I had contemplated sufficiently, to undergo conversion. So I did.

I didn't tell my parents (my grandparents had already passed away) about my intention to convert until about six months before I had my conversion ceremony. They were pretty unhappy about it. However, I was about to graduate from law school and I had just been awarded a postgraduate fellowship in civil rights law at Howard University. So they decided to simply ignore everything about me that sounded "Jewish." I can honestly say that my adopted parents and I never had a conversation about my conversion or about what I had learned through my years of study. Never. It was not a part of my life they wanted to know about.

Not all people with Holocaust memories and an affinity for Judaism or Jews end up converting. Of the one-third of my survey respondents who were born into non-Jewish families, only half of them converted to Judaism as adults.[52] Some respondents, however, have experienced the triple phenomena of Holocaust dreams/memories, feeling like a misfit in their family or society of birth, and feeling innately Jewish or "at home" among Jews, yet have chosen to remain, as the following case calls it, "half-in, half-out" of the Jewish world.

Luuk was born in Rotterdam in 1959 to parents of the Dutch Reformed Church who did not discuss the Holocaust. Growing up, he felt "out of touch" with his family, and had few friends in school. When he was eleven years old, his teacher taught him about what had happened in Holland during World War II. "I was so deeply insulted by it. Angry right down to the core of my being," remembers Luuk. "I am a bad reader, but since then I have read everything about the Holocaust. The strange thing is that I could envision the stories. I *saw* the stories."

In his early twenties, Luuk became a board member of an international organization that held its World Congress in Tel Aviv.

> It was the first time I went to Israel. I stayed there for a week, and I never felt so much at home. I loved it. It was Pesach, and although I am not Jewish, I understood the customs. I noticed that that had to be strange, that without ever having been exposed

---

52. My survey makes no claims to be scientific, as it is a self-selected survey. The first thirty-six responses came as a result of two articles I wrote on the subject published in a Jewish magazine and on a Jewish website. The next eleven responses came through my personal Facebook page. Most of the remaining responses came from people who googled "reincarnation and the Holocaust."

to Jewish Pesach customs, I understood them. But it did not feel strange. After that week, I decided to learn Hebrew. I studied Hebrew for nine years.

Luuk became a schoolteacher. When he started to teach his students about World War II and the persecutions of the Dutch under the Nazis, "the memories returned."

> The camps were vivid and clear memories. I first thought it was because I am a storyteller (teacher), but I realized during one of my lessons that the memory was too clear and too real to be only something that you are telling. It was more something that is part of you.
>
> I felt sick. It made me gasp for air…. Even before I visited Auschwitz, I could see how it was. Those memories have always been there. What exactly do I remember? I saw it happening. I mean it literally. Walking toward the gas chamber, being already inside…. It is gruesome, it is getting suffocated, and it is a part of me that comes out in small spaces and in large crowds. Still. And darkness when it is too hot. That makes me afraid, and that will never go away.

At some point, Luuk started a website about the Jewish history of Amsterdam and Rotterdam, writing about the locations, enterprises, and people before, during, and after the war. He includes brief biographies of local Jews murdered by the Nazis. When he interviews Jewish residents and they start to explain to him about Jewish customs and observances, he feels that he already knows, and that no explanation is necessary.

Recently, Luuk quit his job as a teacher and enrolled in university to study Jewish history. "I want to work as a historian," he notes. "I want to tell the stories. As for the Jewish world, I am half-in, half-out. I know, I see, and I feel. But this place is a good place, getting involved on my own terms. I leave the memories and do what I have to do—to tell the stories."

A strong reaction to anti-Semitism is not necessarily the sign of a Jewish soul, but for Julie Anne Miller it was followed by a vivid flashback. Born in Scotland in 1969, Julie is from the English gypsy community and has lived in Durham, in the northeast of England, for the last twelve years.

> We live in a house, but I have traveled all my life, in Australia, the USA, Germany, etc. I was brought up to believe in God, but was not from a religious home. Our culture (nothing like a popular movie depicts) includes a strong belief in God and Bible, and some superstition.
>
> I started reading the Bible and praying and looking to God for the answers at about the age of thirteen. At eighteen, by which time I was married (at seventeen), I became a born-again Christian. I have always felt a strong bond to the Jewish people but never mixed outside my own culture, so my contact outside was nil, apart from buying or selling.
>
> I went to a gypsy church. (Yes, we have those. The non-gypsy don't really want us in theirs. One

or two they don't mind, but any more is a no-go.) Around four years ago, I started reading the Jewish website Aish.com and got so much from it. I started to feel spiritually starved in the church I was going to. I started questioning them in the church about this belief or that belief. It disturbed me so much.

Around this time, I had a dream. I was in a hotel lobby, and everything was white and everyone was wearing white from head to toe. When I walked up to the desk, the person behind opened a book and asked, "What is your name?"

I said, "Julie Anne Miller."

The person said, "You have another name."

"What is it?"

"It's Rebecca."

Then I woke up. I believe it was God telling me my Hebrew name.

Then came the thing that turned my world upside down. In church I started to hear hostile preaching about the Jewish nation. So I went to the pastor who was saying it, and I said very politely that he was reading the Bible out of context. He then took me in a room with another pastor and shouted at me. I was calm but stood my ground, and repeated from the Scriptures all of God's promises to the Jewish nation.

My husband has never been back to church since that day, but I kept going because I wanted to see what they were teaching people. I thought they were just ignorant, but after more of the same thing, asking them to explain to me with Scripture the reasoning behind this hostile preaching (they couldn't), I left the church. I couldn't understand why no one else was bothered by all this. The pastor obviously had a major problem with the Jewish people. I couldn't fathom why it didn't bother anyone else. I never could understand why the Holocaust didn't bother other people.

The next bit is where it gets very weird, so please bear with me. A word kept coming into my head: *baruck*. So that night I googled it. It's Hebrew for "blessed." Sometime later, I saw, and at the same time felt, a scene. It was extremely vivid. I haven't told anyone except my mother and my two oldest daughters. And whenever I tell it, I get very upset. I just knew they were speaking Yiddish, and it was Warsaw. I am very emotional about it. I can't even talk about it and tell the story without crying.

I saw the scene from the perspective of a little girl of about three. She woke to a loud banging. The bedroom door was open. She had been sleeping with her coat on. Her mother and father were at a table. Her father was wearing a cap. He had been sitting, but he jumped up when men in German uniforms burst in. They shot him. The mother and the little girl (who I knew was called Zelda) were taken with others to the back of a truck. Zelda asked her mother why. In the next scene, they were in what I believe to be gas chambers, undressed. She looked at her mother and asked why. Then it ended.

I knew her name was Zelda. When I heard the name Zelda, I didn't even think it was a name. I knew it was Warsaw, and I knew they spoke Yiddish. It was just something I was aware of as I saw it. The father had a cap on. I didn't know that Jewish men wore a cap inside the house. Non-Jews take their caps off when they enter the house.

By fluke I ended up going to Warsaw the next year, so I visited the Holocaust museum there. We came across a memorial at what used to be the gate of the ghetto. I lit a candle for the little girl, as well as for others. I visited this year again and went back to the same places, but this time I read the names on the memorial. At the very end was the name Zelda.

I have a strong desire to convert to Judaism. I have been in touch with Chabad in Newcastle and Manchester.

In addition to the shortage of Jewish mothers for Jewish souls to come to, I have discovered two other explanations why Jewish souls may come to Christian mothers. The first is that when they were being tortured or killed for being Jews, some people desperately wished they were not Jews. Witness a childhood nightmare of a Chicago-born housewife documented by Yonasson Gershom in his book *Beyond the Ashes*:

I had my coat on with my yellow star, and I was told to take off my coat. So I took off my coat, and even on my dress I had my yellow star. I started to go through the line, and they started writing numbers on us. I remember asking my mother, "Why are they doing this to me? But I've been a good girl."

[Later in the dream]...a soldier came in, and he just said that the children were going to be taken the next day, and we were. We got in a truck and they drove us halfway there, and I remember barbed wire was just about everywhere. And I still didn't know what was going on. This time I was closer to seven [years old]. It didn't really seem like we were there long, but it was too long.... They had furnaces, I remember there were some furnaces that were in buildings, and they were brick, and they were tying some people down, strapping them down, just sticking them in.

They opened up this door of the furnace, and they just started throwing the children in, one after another, and I kept on looking around to see if I could find my brother. I wanted him to hold onto. I couldn't find him anywhere. Soon it came my turn. I kept telling them, "Well, I'll tell you what—I won't be a Jew." I didn't understand what was wrong with being a Jew, but apparently it wasn't good. Didn't help at all.[53]

Such a desire, when facing a torturous death, to not be a Jew could account for being reincarnated as a Christian. That would explain the strange story of Brian Arthur Rish.

---

53. *Beyond the Ashes*, p. 85.

Born in Omaha, Nebraska, in 1977 to a Roman Catholic mother and a Presbyterian father, Brian did not know a single Jew when he was growing up. He had neither knowledge of nor interest in anything Jewish. At the age of twenty-one, he started studying metaphysics and mysticism. One day, he walked into a Barnes and Noble in Columbus, Ohio, and bought a book that delved into six different kinds of mysticism, including Kabbalah.

In the midst of reading the chapter on Kabbalah, Brian had a dream that was to recur frequently for the next two years. In the dream he saw himself as a religious Jew with a beard and sidelocks. He was a scribe, writing on parchment scrolls in a strange language that he later identified as Hebrew. Mysteriously, he was drawing tiny crowns on certain letters. When he would wake up, he would think, *That's crazy! Why would anyone put crowns on letters?* Only years later would he discover that Jewish scribes, when copying sacred texts, do indeed put crowns on letters.[54]

In the second part of the recurring dream, he saw himself being ushered into a shower room with many other Jewish men. He knew that the showers were really gas chambers. As he was going into the room, he was trying to understand why this was happening to him. He had been a devout Jew, who had fought to make sure that his children married Jews. Now he was angry at God for his bitter fate. "Right as they were about to turn on the showers," he recalls, "I dropped to my knees and said, with as much anger and hatred as I could muster, 'God, why couldn't You have made me a gentile?'"

---

54. In sacred Jewish scrolls, crowns are drawn on certain letters: שעטנזגץ.

At the end of 2001, while the dream was still recurring, Brian went to a Jewish chat room. He started chatting with an Orthodox Jew who called himself "Bnei Torah." Within three months, Brian abandoned Christianity. Two years later, he started the conversion process through the Chicago Rabbinical Council, the closest Orthodox rabbinical court to Omaha. In 2010, Brian moved to Israel. In November 2011, he officially converted, taking the name Yitzchak.

What did he take away from his recurring dream of the angry *sofer* (scribe) who wanted to be a gentile? "The only thing I could really take from the dream is not to turn against God," says Yitzchak. "When I turned against God, my life got worse. Now I know it's my job to not turn against God." Yitzchak currently lives in the town of Yavniel in northern Israel. He is learning to be a *sofer*. And he puts crowns on letters.

The other possibility why a Jewish soul may "choose" to be born in a non-Jewish family is the shame at having cooperated with the Nazis, making the soul feel unworthy of being part of the Jewish people. Such is the case of John, born to a Baptist family in Atlanta, Georgia, in 1957.

At the age of twelve, John had "a horrifying and life-defining experience." He woke up in a cold sweat, screaming from a nightmare that would recur frequently during the following years and decades. Forty years later, in describing his dream, he wrote: "If it is 'only a dream,' I'm at a loss to explain why it has haunted me these forty-plus years, how so many elements have been shown accurate beyond my knowledge at the time I first began experiencing it, and why so many people who have heard or read this account affirm that it rings true for them."

The nightmare, which to him seemed real, had four parts. In the first part he is an adolescent, huddled with other people on the landing of a staircase. The stench of urine is overwhelming. In the distance he hears the sound of the scratching and whimpering of dogs. He is afraid to make a sound. He hears the metallic screech of brakes, then feet running, and women crying out.

> All of these sounds are growing louder and drawing closer. I don't move. My body is trembling almost uncontrollably, sweat is streaming down my face. It burns my eyes, but I will not move. I must not! Now I hear the gruff shouts and commands of the soldiers, and my heart is pounding. *God!* I silently scream. But He does not reply.

Soldiers are banging on the door below. One of their group stands up on trembling legs, descends the staircase, and opens the door latch. He is immediately shot in the forehead. While the dogs remain outside with their handlers, the soldiers rush up the stairs.

> Suddenly rough hands yank me upward by the right arm.... The German spits something at me that I don't understand, then adds, *"Jetzt maden!"* (Now, maggots!) My left arm is locked tightly to the man huddled at my side. The soldier

yanks hard a second time, and my grip gives way.

Then he feels himself in the back of an open truck. The dream goes black.

The second part of the dream is the most gruesome:

> I'm pulling a wooden cart. Sometimes I push it. The floor is uneven and slick. I must not fall, I tell myself as my right ankle suddenly threatens to buckle. The pain brings me back to fuller consciousness. I start to wipe the sweat from my eyes with one hand, but the cart begins to tilt, and I quickly regain control. I need to pause, but my feet refuse to stop, and I continue onward. Stopping is not an option in any case.
>
> The cart is filled with wood. Some pieces are long, some are short, they are all very thin. I am pushing or pulling the cart because it is to be pushed or pulled…. Not being noticed is the way of survival. How long have I been doing this essential work? A day? A week? A year? Nothing matters except the cart being moved and maintaining my pace and the wood being delivered to the place it must go. This is essential work…. I am pushing or pulling the cart to its designated destination and that is all. I care nothing for the wood, and even less for the fire it feeds….
>
> My head must always be bowed. That too is essential, and I am learning. Life is pushing or pulling, my arms are aching, my shoulders are screaming,

my head is bowed, but the cart is always moving and that is life for me. It is enough.

It is verboten, but sometimes I glance up and see other people pushing similar carts. Some of them are young like me and some are older. Everyone here is male. There is so much wood to be moved that it takes many strong men, and I am a man. Of course, men like me don't matter, but the carts do, and men push the carts.

My stomach heaves, but I force it back down without missing a step. There is something bad about the wood in the carts, something unclean. Don't look in the carts! … I care nothing for the wood, whether it is burned or not. Caring is the way of death.

We all dress in the same dingy clothing, and we do not question why we push the wood. There are cords and cords of the bad wood to be pushed in the carts to the fires that never go out because that is what is to be done with the unclean wood… except…I know it isn't wood in the carts at all.

I turn and resume pushing the cart. But as I do, another cart passes and a lifeless arm is dangling from its side and there is a scream (from me?) and then….

In the next part of the dream, he is standing, embarrassed, in front of a large, gray desk. There is a giant of a man sitting behind the desk.

He will demand to know, but I cannot (allow myself to) remember what he surely already knows. I can only remember the wood that I pushed and no, it was not a hand.... Surely it was bad wood only, wood does not have hands.... It was not a hand, and I feel ashamed at what I will not know, at what I refuse to know. But, you see, if I knew, how could I ever remain alive? What will I tell him? Why is he silent, staring at me with obvious disgust as if I was a piece of wood? A piece of thin wood.... Say something!

But truly I do know what I did: I did whatever they told me to do. I do know that it was wrong to push the carts of wood and I do feel ashamed for it, but.... My heart is breaking, my jaw is clenched, my throat is contracting. My inward parts are shifting upward into my throat. I force myself to stand still before the desk and to be a man.

Oh! how can I ever be forgiven? By God or by man! This much I know: I am damned.

The last part of the dream is reminiscent of the end of a death march, when, facing defeat, the Germans evacuated the camps and forced the prisoners to walk until most of them died.

In the distance I see trees, a beautiful forest. So lovely and cool. I peer. There is a path there.... That path is so lovely and cool. If only I could reach that path I would run forever, and no one would ever see me again until I reached...the Holy Land! Surely the path leads there. But...but I cannot reach the path. And even if I could, I am not worthy to tread upon it, because of what I did, because of what I have abandoned, because of what I have forgotten, and because of the bad wood.... And because I am damned, mostly that, because I am cut off from my people. I am beyond forgiveness. But still, I look at the cool trees and the path and I sigh.

My legs ache and tremble in the burning sun. I glance down at my right foot. It is inflamed and swollen. Most of my body has become dangerously thin, thinner, for I was never large. My ribs show through my skin, but at least I'm not hungry anymore—I have left such luxuries as hunger behind— Now, I am hunger itself. My ankle is bloated and throbbing. Why am I here?...

I glance up at the pit that lies before us, between us and the cool forest and the trail, and it is then that I realize why I am so dirty and why my hands are bleeding. I remember what I have done for them...before...and now.... What they made me do...but still, what I did, and I know that even God could never forgive me now.[55]

Shortly after the onset of the dreams, which John considered actual memories, he left the Baptist Church and dedicated himself to finding truth. As an adult, he traveled throughout the world, studied various religions, and earned an MA in

---

55. Rabbi Shlomo Nachman ben Ya'acov, "My Shoah Memories," www.allfaith.com.

religious studies and an interfaith counseling degree. "I also studied Judaism on and off," he testifies, "but it terrified me due to my sense of unworthiness.... Eventually, having looked everywhere I could think of, I decided I could no longer deny who I had always known I was, a Jew."

John and his wife converted to Judaism in 2013. But a sense of guilt and unworthiness still plagued him. From his dreams, it was clear to him that in his previous life he had been a Sonderkommando in Auschwitz, cooperating with the Nazi murder machine by taking the corpses from the gas chambers to the crematoria. Even though he had been a mere teenager, his resistance worn down during his time in hiding, his moral repugnance at what he had done shadowed him throughout this lifetime.

The waters of the mikveh, the ritual bath that is an essential step in Jewish conversion, had expunged most of the stain on his soul, but something still made him feel unworthy to be a Jew.

A couple of weeks after the mikveh, my wife and I went to Israel for seven weeks. The first time I saw the Kotel [the Western Wall], my knees buckled, and I began to sweat profusely. My wife was concerned and suggested we return to our hotel. I said no, that I had to go down and touch the Kotel. I told her that I believed (and I sincerely did) that for doing such a thing Hashem might strike me dead. I wanted her to know in advance. I approached the Wall slowly, with my hands out, and a strong energy of love flowed from the stones to my hands.

As I finally touched the Kotel, I began to sob, and then I knew that my *tikkun* [rectification] was complete. I stood there for a couple of hours—praying, crying, and feeling the stone. I sensed that the path from my dream ended at the Kotel and that I had finally arrived.[56]

---

56. From an email to the author, December 13, 2017.

PART II

TIKKUN

CHAPTER 9

VICTORIES: VANQUISHING THE DEMONS OF THE PAST

THE PURPOSE OF THE SOUL'S DESCENT to the physical world is, according to Kabbalah, *tikkun* or rectification of past mistakes. Just as every soul is unique, so every *tikkun* is unique, as illustrated by the stories in this and the following chapter.

For some, such as Junie Maggio, a failure of action can be rectified through a single, glorious choice. For others, *tikkun* is a rectification of a character flaw; fear must be replaced by courage, selfishness by generosity. For still others, the disposition of anger—at God and at human beings—must be rectified by the soul-soothing serum of faith and love. Some, like Sara David below, find themselves suddenly facing their *tikkun* almost by happenstance. For Yael Shahar, it took twenty-nine years of searching to find the door to her *tikkun* and two more years to unlock it. Yet, as her story shows, *tikkun* is always possible—even for the worst crimes, such as aiding and abetting mass murder.

Whether a person discerns her *tikkun* early in life or it dawns on her only decades later, one inevitably will be vouchsafed the clues that point to the work that must be done. As Dr. Sabine Lucas wrote in her book *Past Life Dreamwork*:

> I...have to confess that I never had any control over the past life dream process that is recorded in this book. The spontaneous return of unconscious memories happens when a person is ready, regardless of whether he or she likes it. I personally decided, after having one particularly uncomfortable dream, that I had better accept what was happening to me, because otherwise I might miss the whole purpose of my life.[57]

Reincarnation replaces the fear of mortality with the assurance of immortality. This immortality has nothing to do with the youthfulness or fitness of the body. The body and all its accoutrements will indeed perish. Reincarnation, however, guarantees the eternal longevity of one's core identity—the soul. Like a child who gets off a roller coaster ride and runs to get in line to do the ride again, our souls crave "another ride," another chance to redress wrongs with clearer consciousness and more benevolent actions. Death comes with a ticket for another ride—although usually the line is very long.

---

57. Lucas, *Past Life Dreamwork*, p. 14.

Sara David suffered in an abusive marriage. Even after she obtained her divorce, she was embroiled in a bitter custody battle that required her to fly from her home in Florida to Chicago, where the litigation was taking place. Born in New York in 1965 to a Jewish family with no connection to the Holocaust, Sara had traveled all over the world, especially to Israel, where she had taken Israeli citizenship at the age of eighteen. She had always loved flying. But at this point in her life, she developed a mysterious phobia.

When she would stand in the Jetway waiting to board the plane, she would have a panic attack, feeling that she was standing in line to enter the gas chamber.

> I was sure that we were all going to die, entering that box, that giant boxcar of bodies, and yet I couldn't warn anyone nor stop it. I got sick, shook uncontrollably with my heart racing, crying and fainting. But I kept flying, because my children depended on it. I asked everyone for help. I took pills to relax. Nothing really helped. Flight attendants hugged me and gave me water, human comforts along the journey.

On the flight that would prove to be a turning point in her life, Sara was sitting in her assigned seat in the back of the plane before takeoff. A kind flight attendant, seeing her panic, asked if he could help her. Gazing at all the people in front of her, whom she saw as "soon-to-be-dead bodies," she told the flight attendant that it would help if she could sit closer to the front of the plane. Soon the flight attendant returned and informed her that there was a seat for her in first class, that a generous couple sitting there, hearing of her need, had invited her to sit with them.

Sara made her way forward, and the attendant showed her where to sit. The couple were German, clearly wealthy, and in their seventies. Sara keenly felt their social superiority to her, how they, of "the German elite," had deigned to help her, the needy passenger from economy class. "I realized," remembers Sara, "that they had invited me to sit with them based upon noblesse oblige, their proper upbringing, and generosity to those less fortunate."

Sara sat next to the woman, who benignly tried to help her relax by engaging her in pleasant conversation, asking her about the best spas, golf courses, and shopping areas in Florida.

> I started to get involved in the conversation but was still reeling with fear and dizziness. Then she took out a book to read, first asking me if I had a book of my own to read. I did. I pulled out *Nine Gates to the Chassidic Mysteries* by Jiří Langer, and proceeded to answer her polite interest in its subject matter. I told her that it is a travelogue from pre–World War II of an assimilated Czech Jew who traveled east throughout Galicia in order to understand firsthand the spirituality of the Chassidim of Eastern Europe.
>
> Her response stunned me. She said that the Jewish people are unbelievable how once again they are rising in power to destroy the world and all its progress, just as they had nearly done to Germany.

With that blatant expression of German anti-Semitism, Sara blacked out for a few moments. When she regained consciousness, she felt like she had died and come back. She was aware that this was no chance encounter. God had arranged this meeting, this face-to-face encounter with a high-ranking, Jew-hating German, in order to give her an opportunity to do what she had failed to do in her previous lifetime. She faced a choice. She could shrink away and obsequiously return to her seat in economy, or she could stand up and defend her people.

She suddenly became aware that she was not a Jew overpowered by the Third Reich, about to die. She was alive, and had, through the shadowy mists of time, survived as a Jew, in a new place and new period. She was not a prisoner of her past. She broke through the bars of her fear, and was free.

With this realization came another that switched their roles. She had thought that this wealthy German woman was the benefactor and she was the almost submissive recipient of her largesse. But once liberated from her fear, Sara sensed a new mission.

> Although it might appear that this woman was here to help me, I suddenly felt that truly I was here to help her. She had a soul buried in such darkness! She had been living in complete darkness and evil lies her entire life—comfortable, luxurious darkness to be sure, just as her noble family's evil lies and history in Germany went back generations. Yet she was actually somewhat engaged in dialogue with me on that flight, in first class, thanks to her generosity towards me in my neediness at that time. Her

soul had reached out towards mine. I had to reach into her worldview and open her eyes to my truth.

I told her that she was mistaken. I told her that I was Jewish, and Israeli. I told her about all the gifts she enjoys daily that are thanks to Israeli inventiveness. I told her about the loving-kindness and sweet simplicity revealed in the book I was reading about Jews in Europe before World War II.

The German woman was shocked, but remained polite. She listened to Sara's assertions, and argued with them. Sara stood her ground. She defended the Jewish people and Israel.

Apparently, Sara won the argument, because the German woman wrote down the names of the author and the book, and promised to find the book in German in order to read it.

Sara also won in a more significant way. After this encounter, her fear of flying disappeared completely. She testifies, "I also seem to have less fear in general now, even when faced with potentially frightening circumstances." Her only regret is that she didn't thank the German woman for participating in her cure.

Most souls from the Holocaust are, quite naturally, reborn with anger, fear, and a sense of grievance. Awareness of reincarnation itself can provide an antidote to these crippling feelings. As Sara David in the above account realized at the critical moment when she was facing a German anti-Semite, she was alive and had, from a higher perspective, survived her own terrible death. Anger, fear, and a sense of grievance over the past can be banished by the visceral awareness of the current, inevitably better, reality.

Such was the experience of Devora Sinton. Born to a Jewish family in California in 1975, Devora was plagued throughout her life by panic attacks and intense grief. Although her great-grandparents had been murdered in the Holocaust and her grandfather had narrowly escaped, Devora attributes the ghosts that tyrannized her life to her own past experience.

> I've had hundreds of panic attacks related to the Holocaust.... Waking up in the middle of the night not being able to breathe.... Feeling like I was dying alone.... Many images of the gas chambers and bodies on the floor, or feeling that my child had been taken away from me, for many, many years. Unbearable endless pain and grief that feels like it has been stuck in every cell of my body.
>
> I have cried what feels like millions of hours over the past twenty years. I had many years of unbelievable pain, guilt, and rage towards the Nazis and towards God (and towards myself for the belief that I had to abandon a baby that died). The pain over the years was as real and strong as if the Nazis were standing in front of me.

Throughout the years, Devora felt like her soul did not want to be in this world, and she struggled to "ground my soul in my body." She eventually found some salvation through dance. She developed and now teaches women a program she calls "Dance Journeys," which combines movement, meditation, and Jewish concepts.

> I have seen my own past-life story over the years. I believe that I was a Jewish Communist. I believe that I died in the gas chambers, hating God and the Nazis with hatred that one cannot believe one can even hold inside oneself. I wanted to kill and take revenge. I spent sometimes eight hours a day digging in the trenches, trying to get out of that hatred and anger. This voice kept coming down: *You're just hurting yourself by holding onto this rage.*

A major turning point for Devora came after she and her husband moved to Israel in 2005, taking up residence in Jerusalem. On Israel's Holocaust Day in 2017, Devora decided to take the light-rail to the Kotel (Western Wall), Israel's holiest place of prayer. On the train, when an attendant checked her ticket, Devora had a Holocaust flashback, an almost routine experience for her.

Some fifteen minutes later, she reached the top of the steps leading to the Kotel Plaza. She looked down and saw the plaza filled with Jews. The contrast struck her like lightning. It was Holocaust Day, commemorating the Germans' fiendish enterprise to exterminate all Jews, yet here they were—masses of proud Jews—living in their Biblical homeland. *Wow!* Devora marveled. *We're alive and we're back home.*

What Devora experienced that day was not just the continuity of the Jewish people, but also her own continuity, through reincarnation. Later, she would write in her journal, "I know now that this cruel, lonely death was not my end point, as physical death does not mean finality."

An even more incisive realization was that it was the pain itself that led her to the evolved spiritual state she now enjoys:

> I personally do not feel like I would be here in Israel doing exactly what I want to be doing as part of the Jewish people (including raising three holy souls in this land) without the deep, constant, daily discomfort my soul experienced for the past twenty years. Each discomfort pushed through a new soul truth, which eventually landed me home in Jerusalem.
>
> I also do energy healing. I remember all those years when I felt like I was literally in the trenches of working through the pain, underneath my blanket just praying that Hashem would make me a messenger to help others with the wisdom I was accessing through the depths of this suffering. And now almost exclusively in my healing practice, I have people who are drawn to my work who themselves have had many torturous past-life experiences. I feel like every client was hand-chosen to come my way, as I now have the vessel to support this depth of healing in others. It is as if Hashem really heard my request from underneath the covers.

Devora believes that in her Holocaust lifetime she was a Communist, and she died in the gas chambers hating God.

Asked what is her rectification in this lifetime, Devora replied:

> I believe my *tikkun* is to be religious in this lifetime,
> to come to know Hashem's presence in my life, and
> to be able to help *Am Yisrael* and the world to find
> and experience the presence of Hashem.
>
> One of the last pieces that is integrating within me
> is the feeling that Hashem really loves me so much
> (which was clearly hard to feel in that lifetime), and
> with that how much I love Hashem. As I am integrat-
> ing this piece, it feels like all the last bits of pain are
> leaving, as no pain can really hold in a place where
> you experience this deep sense of love.[58]

While Devora Sinton spent twenty years of inner work
achieving her *tikkun*, Junie Maggio affected her *tikkun* by a
single life-changing choice.

Junie was born into a Catholic family in Prairie Village, a
suburb of Kansas City, Missouri, in 1952. Prairie Village was,
as Junie describes it, "where all the ethnic people lived." Her
neighborhood was 80 percent Jewish, and all of Junie's friends
were Jewish.

When she was in first grade in Catholic school, the mon-
signor consigned Junie to hell, because she had committed
the "mortal sin" of missing a Sunday mass. "I reasoned,"
remembers Junie, "that since the Church taught that all

---

58. Interview with Devora Sinton, January 23, 2018.

others who were not Christian were going to hell, I would be together with all the Jews from the neighborhood and all would be well for me. My Jewish friends would love me in hell, and I would be okay."

Although no one in her neighborhood talked about the Holocaust, starting from an early age and throughout her life, Junie has been obsessed with the subject. This obsession was accompanied by a feeling of guilt.

> I just had this hatred for all things German. The very words *Germany, Nazi, Hitler*, the sight of a swastika, would send shivers up my spine. I could not abide the word *concentration* because it meant "concentration camp" to me. The only place I felt really spiritually safe was with Jewish people. I have been this way all of my life. I think about the Holocaust often, sometimes daily. Whereas I have Jewish friends who think like I do in this context, I have never met another gentile who thinks and feels the way I do.
>
> I do remember feeling guilty when I was little for being alive and for living in a wonderful home with nice parents, friends, and a wonderful neighborhood. I felt so ashamed that I lived while millions had died. I remember looking up at some Christian symbols and thinking, "Had I lived then, I would not have stayed silent. I would have done something! I know I would have done something to help." I felt deep, deep guilt and terrible shame in being alive and for having a good life. All of my life, my mantra

was "If I had lived then, I would have done something to help."

The *tikkun* that would wipe away Junie's guilt for presumably failing to save lives during the Holocaust presented itself when she was forty-two years old. She read an article entitled "A Question of Duty," written by Steven Mosher.

> The article was about the methodical killing of unwanted baby girls due to China's one-child policy. There was an editorial comment at the end of the article that said something to the effect of reports of the widespread killing of infant baby girls is like the scattered reports coming out of Europe in 1938 about the methodical killing of Jews. My blood ran cold. My immediate thought was *This is my chance. I will not be silent. I will intervene. I will help.* So I adopted my first daughter from China in 1996 and my second one in 2001.

After adopting her Chinese daughters—literally saving their lives—Junie's lifelong guilt ebbed away. Of course, the choice to adopt a child may take just a moment, but the ramifications of that choice—raising a child—takes years of committed effort. A failure to act can be rectified by action. Simple math, difficult life choice.

Sometimes a person has an intuitive recognition of who she might have been in her former lifetime, and this points to the direction of her *tikkun*. Nicolette Verhoeven was born in Amsterdam in 1958 to a Christian family who defined themselves as humanists. Like many of her European contemporaries, Nicolette was drawn to New Age beliefs and practices. After getting a degree in psychology, she discovered Re-evaluation Counseling, an international movement founded by Harvey Jackins. Re-evaluation Counseling utilizes a method of reciprocal counseling based on the recollection of psychological and physical traumas accompanied by various types of emotional catharsis. Jackins taught that a child growing up is socialized as either the oppressor or the oppressed. Either role is painful; one can release the pain through discharging it (expressing it physically) in a workshop setting.

Nicolette was both white (oppressor) and a woman (oppressed). A former feminist, she didn't want to be an oppressor. So, in her late twenties, she began attending weekend workshops. Each workshop centered on one form of oppression: blacks by whites, women by men, or Jews by non-Jews. After attending other workshops, Nicolette decided to do the Jew/non-Jew workshop. She was, of course, assigned to the non-Jewish cohort.

The exercises are geared to arouse emotions in order to work through them, but Nicolette felt no emotions as the non-Jewish "oppressor." Then the subject of the Holocaust was raised. Nicolette burst into tears and cried inconsolably, but as the victim rather than as the oppressor. A Jew in the group suggested that perhaps Nicolette had Jewish ancestry and should be in the Jewish cohort. As she recalls what happened next:

> There I started feeling a thousand things. Mostly a lot of fear, and a lot of sadness. I cried a lot. The sessions work in pairs, where one is feeling and the other is in the here-and-now and is helping. I felt like there was a long tunnel in front of me that I was afraid of going into. The helper encouraged me to enter. I went in, and on the other side I saw barbed wire. I felt a great fear. I felt like a three-year-old child. I felt that I wanted to run away from there. The helper worked on those feelings with me.

In truth, Nicolette did have a Jewish ancestor. She could trace her family tree back eight generations to the 1700s, to a Jewish woman from Portugal who had married a Dutch Christian man named Verhoeven. When she wrote this information to the man who had suggested she join the Jewish cohort, he wrote back, "Welcome home." Reading those words, Nicolette shed tears.

During the period that followed, Nicolette embarked on a journey of Jewish exploration that eventually, fifteen years later, led her to convert to Judaism. On the first Rosh HaShanah after her workshop epiphany, she attended services at a local Amsterdam synagogue. "The sound of the shofar," recalls Nicolette, "pulled my soul from somewhere far away right into my body. It made me cry. I fled to the bathroom and cried for half an hour before I could return to the service. I felt that there must be something such as a Jewish soul, and I must be one."

A low-grade fear had always hovered in the background of Nicolette's childhood. She feels that her *tikkun* in this lifetime is to overcome fear. This includes the fear of being Jewish, with all of the suffering that has been inflicted on Jews in the past and could again arise in the future. "I was in my forties when I converted," declares Nicolette. "I felt that part of my *tikkun* was to have the courage to become Jewish again."

Nicolette (by then calling herself Navah) was forty-eight and living in Israel when a Dutch friend suggested they go together to Yad Vashem. Navah resisted; she did not want to go. But her friend encouraged her, and Navah summoned the courage to face her fears. Her friend led her into the Children's Memorial, a large, dimly lit hall where a candle reflected in a myriad of mirrors represents the one and a half million Jewish children murdered by the Nazis. The only sound echoing in this silent chamber is a recording of the names of each child, with her birthplace and her age at the time of her death.

Navah and her friend sat there for a long time. Unexpectedly, Navah startled, as if being called. "Suddenly I heard my name, Nicole. She was from Lyon, France, and had died at the age of three. I felt at that moment that something came back to me and fell into place. I felt, *This is me.*"

Navah is presently living in Jerusalem's Jewish Quarter and has recently worked with a Kabbalistic rabbi to heal that inner child. This work involved overcoming fear and also learning to trust God. She explains:

> I didn't trust God at all because of my Holocaust trauma. I felt that God didn't want me to be happy, that He wanted to punish me and hurt me. The spiritual work I am doing—to heal the three-year-old Nicole—is helping me learn to trust God. In the

last few months it's becoming clearer how God is guiding my life and giving me gifts. For example, it's a miracle that I found an apartment in the Jewish Quarter for a great price, an apartment with two rooms and light, just what I wanted. I've been able to feel God's hand a lot lately; it's really strong. I now know that God wants me to be happy. That's a big part of my *tikkun*.

An interesting side note to Navah's story is that she wonders whether her soul is reincarnated from that seventeenth-century Portuguese Jewish ancestor who chose to marry a Christian and convert to his faith. Most of the Jews in Amsterdam during that period had fled from the Spanish Inquisition, which had extended its tentacles into Portugal in 1536, or were the children of those fugitives. Navah speculates that her Jewish ancestor, traumatized by the Inquisition, which burned at the stake everyone discovered to be practicing Judaism, probably converted to the safety of Christianity out of fear. "Bringing myself back to Judaism in this lifetime," remarks Navah, "is also a *tikkun* for my Portuguese ancestor."

Is Nicolette really the reincarnation of the three-year-old French Nicole? Does it matter? The intuitive sense that one is the reincarnation of a particular person who was killed in the Holocaust often gives direction to one's *tikkun*, regardless of whether that speculation is accurate.

Such is the case of Janet Kasten Friedman, who was born into a Jewish family in New York in 1953. Janet's father was a Holocaust survivor who fought with the Bielski partisans.

Her father and her American-born mother did not discuss the Holocaust when she was growing up, except in Yiddish or in whispers when they thought that their daughter could not hear. Janet, whose Hebrew name is Yiddis, was named for her father's little brother Yiddle, who was killed as a child in the Holocaust.

Janet acknowledges that her recurring dream throughout her lifetime of being shot in the back while running away ("It hurt and I died") may have derived from the whispered story of Yiddle's death that she heard from her parents. Also, the panic attacks and depression she suffered after the 2005 expulsion of Jewish settlers from Gush Katif may have been an inherited trauma.

> The disengagement from Gush Katif triggered a panic attack in me. The sight of Jews being rounded up and driven from their homes was intolerable to me. I suffered from depression that was just barely above clinical levels, for *years*! The muscles in my neck, shoulders, pectorals were in such spasm that I could barely move my head right-left to cross the street. The pain radiated throughout my body. For a year or two I just waited for it to go away. I avoided seeing doctors who would prescribe serious medication or surgery, because I knew that it was of psychological origin.
>
> My "narrative" has included a *need* to make aliyah, a goal that was my top priority and that I achieved right after high school. The "bonus" goal was a search for greater authenticity, which I achieved by becoming *baalat teshuvah* [Orthodox].

Doing this has made me very happy. I saw this as a kind of victory over Hitler. I came to see my life as a reincarnation of "little Yiddle." He had nothing; I have everything! He never got to grow up; I am living a long and healthy life! Yiddle's parents died when he was a baby, even before the war; my parents saw me and my kids into adulthood! Yiddle was a helpless Jew; I am an Israeli! Yiddle got little pleasure in his life; I get a lot of pleasure. I believe that I am living with double intensity...once for myself and once for Yiddle.

I have, of course, no proof of this. I don't feel a need for it. I'm allowed to have my own narrative.

Helen Epstein, in her book *Children of the Holocaust: Conversations with Sons and Daughters of Survivors,* reported that many children of survivors had the feeling of being followed around by "ghosts" of their dead family members, or of being proxies for the lives of those who had been killed.[59] We may conjecture, based on Kabbalah, that these children of survivors are the actual reincarnated souls of their murdered relatives, but there is obviously no way to distinguish between the two phenomena. While Janet herself makes no claims of certitude that she is Yiddle, she feels that the choices she has made in her life have redeemed his truncated existence.

Indeed, the Satmar Rebbe, Rav Yoel Teitelbaum, himself a Holocaust survivor and the leader of a Chassidic community of tens of thousands, admonished his followers to treat their

59. Helen Epstein, *Children of the Holocaust* (New York: G. P. Putnam's Sons, 1979).

children well because some of them were the reincarnated souls of their own murdered parents.[60]

After my article about reincarnation, "The Chapter After," appeared in *Ami Magazine,* a reader sent a letter to the editor: "While a few years ago I may have laughed off that particular article as nonsense, I have a personal anecdote to share that has proven that this idea of souls being reborn from previous Holocaust victims could be very real."

She went on to report how before their son was born, she and her husband had already chosen a name for him. However, the day before the brit, her husband learned something about his paternal great-great-grandfather Yehoshua, who had perished in the Holocaust. They decided to name their son Yehoshua for this murdered ancestor.

When the child was four and a half years old, his mother decided, as part of his bedtime ritual, to sing every night a different melody for the iconic song *"Ani Maamin,"* expressing yearning for the coming of Mashiach (the Messiah). One night she sang a tune that was attributed to Azriel David Fastag, who composed the melody on the train to Auschwitz. When she started singing, little Yehoshua piped up, "Mommy, this is the train *Ani Maamin.*"

> Shocked that he would have known this story at such a young age, I asked him if anyone had told him the story surrounding this particular song. Surely someone must have mentioned this story, but who would tell such a little boy such a heavy

---

60. Quoted by Rabbi Fischel Schachter, who heard it from students of the Satmar Rebbe, email to the author, February 1, 2021.

story? He answered, "No, why? What story?"

I then asked him why he called this "the train *Ani Maamin.*"

He replied, "When you sang this song, I thought of a bunch of people stuffed on a train, so I'm calling it the train *Ani Maamin.*"

While this account strongly suggests that young Yehoshua may be the reincarnation of his murdered ancestor, identifying one's past incarnation is only the first step. Knowing who one may have been in one's previous incarnation may point in the direction of one's *tikkun,* but the work must still be done.

Mysteriously, Kabbalah teaches that if a soul descends to this physical world and occupies a fetus in the womb of its mother for a minimum of thirty days, then that soul has accomplished a *tikkun.* The esoteric concept is that for some exalted souls merely descending from the spiritual realms to the physical world is in itself so difficult that it may constitute a sufficient *tikkun* for those who have nothing else to rectify. For many religious Jewish women, this mystical concept is a real consolation for them when they have a stillborn baby.

Dr. Naomi Greenwald, PhD, wrote her doctoral dissertation on the topic of how Orthodox Jewish women experienced the loss of a stillborn baby. Some findings that emerged from her interviews showed how mothers conceptualized the baby as briefly descending to this earth in order to rectify something from a past lifetime. As Dr. Greenwald described her research in an email to me:

> The mothers I interviewed perceived their baby as a holy soul that required a brief sojourn into this world in order to obtain a *tikkun* for some small wrongdoing from a past lifetime. Despite the pain of the experience, they saw themselves as fortunate in having been able to serve as the conduit for the soul's completion of its mission through the pregnancy, and this made the experience meaningful, rather than a senseless tragedy.
>
> Several mothers talked about how their perception of their baby's soul as exceptionally elevated affected their behaviors in the aftermath of the loss. For example, one mother discussed how she realized that something was wrong when her baby stopped moving. She dressed up in her Shabbat clothes to go to the ultrasound, where she knew she would receive bad news, since she saw it as an elevated moment, and wanted to be dressed appropriately. Mothers also discussed how the loss of their baby helped to strengthen their belief in the immortality of the soul, in *techiyat hameitim* [the revival of the dead], and in the idea that every person comes into this world for a purpose.

Many people discover their *tikkun* seemingly by happenstance, when the circumstances of their lives present them with a choice that turns out to be fateful. They are like a person looking for shells on the beach when the waves throw up a gold necklace. Rare is the person like Yael Shahar, who for decades actively searched for her *tikkun* with a one-pointed focus, like a person combing the beach for a missing pill that will cure her of a painful malady. Even when she found the treasure map (in the form of a wise rabbi) that would lead her to her *tikkun*, she had to dig for it during two years of arduous effort.

Born as Leanne Wesley to a Christian Texan family in 1962, from the age of nine (her mother says even before), she had nightmares and flashbacks for which she had no context. How did such horrid images invade the young mind of a Texan girl whose chief love was horses? Leanne was in high school and on her way to her dream job of training horses when the car radio played a song that would change her life.

> I flip through the channels...and stop.
>
> A melody from beyond any dream or nightmare flows from the old Caddy's excellent sound system. I am in the place from before the nightmares. My hand caresses salt sea, chasing tiny fish as waves stain my rolled-up trousers.... Too soon, the music ends. A perky voice chimes in over the last notes, unforgivably spoiling the mood, bringing me back to the smell of pecan trees and the Texas springtime. "That's all for this week's Jewish Music Hall. Join us Tuesday for our annual fundraising drive. Come out and show your support!"

Numbly, I memorize the number to call to volunteer. I have to find the name of that song! Some part of me was stolen, somewhere, sometime, and that song is a clue. And so Tuesday morning finds me in Dallas, having braved the perils of the Texas Highway Patrol in pursuit of a song. I make new friends, some of whom invite me to visit the new Jewish community center in Fort Worth. "But I'm not Jewish," I say.

Or maybe I don't. Maybe I'm simply too overwhelmed to say anything at all. Nonetheless, I begin to read and to question: "I'm not Jewish, am I?" More reading, and the answer seems to be: "Yes, perhaps I am, after all." Something deep inside breathes a sigh of relief, a murmur of resignation, a hint of sorrow and fear...and a hope so shocking in its raw pain that it must be shut out completely. But another Voice whispers quietly in my ear: "Welcome home! I've missed you."

The Orthodox conversion, two years down the line, will be merely the rubber stamp on a choice never really made at all. And so I set out on a treasure hunt, to find that missing part of myself stolen by something, somewhere...and hidden in a song.[61]

Taking the Hebrew name Yael, she went to Israel for the first time at the age of nineteen, after a year and a half of college majoring in physics. Two years later she moved to Israel

---

61. Yael Shahar, "The Revival of the Dead: A Personal Journey," January 2017, https://www.yaelshahar.com/revival-dead-personal-journey/.

for good. She volunteered for a first response unit, then the police sniper unit, and then the reserves. Professionally, she became a respected counterterrorism expert. "Looking back," Yael remarks, "it seems clear that all of that was an attempt to make amends, to rebuild my sense of self-worth, and above all to keep the Holocaust from happening again."

What was the great sin that needed such assiduous amends? The flashbacks, constant and tortured, sucked her into the life of a Jewish boy from Salonika named Ovadya, who at the age of seventeen was deported to Auschwitz-Birkenau along with his family and most of the other Jews of Salonika. His family was gassed immediately, but Ovadya's fate was worse than death. He was assigned to the Sonderkommandos, the Jewish prisoners responsible for taking the dead bodies out of the gas chambers and moving them to the crematoria. After that, his job was to remove the bones and grind them up.

Yael was leading a double life. Married and a respected professional, she was consumed by the horrific, detailed memories of Ovadya. At some point, she was diagnosed as suffering from post-traumatic stress disorder. But how did the traumas enter Yael's mind and soul? In her riveting memoir, *Returning*, Yael Shahar describes the decades of her struggle with ghastly memories not her own. Only once does she mention the idea—offered by her husband—that she might be a reincarnation of Ovadya.

More than the source of her tormented memories, Yael was haunted by two questions: What should Ovadya have done? And what could Ovadya/Yael do now as a *tikkun*?

Eventually, twenty-nine years after coming to Israel, Yael took these two questions to a rabbi, whom she calls Rabbi Ish-Shalom. Halachah holds that in order to save one's own life, one can trespass any commandments of the Torah except for murder, adultery, and idolatry. Yael, speaking for Ovadya, maintained that, since the Jews who were killed in the gas chambers would have died anyway, he was innocent, but he wanted to know how authoritative Jewish sources would judge him.

For two tumultuous years, Yael studied the sources with Rav Ish-Shalom, as more incriminating details of Ovadya's complicity with the German murder machine made their way out of Yael's unconscious mind. In addition to removing bodies from the gas chambers, she discovered that Ovadya had also assisted, albeit indirectly, in murdering Jews. Finally, the rabbi issued his ruling: Ovadya was guilty. He should have allowed himself to be killed rather than cooperate with the Nazis.

As for what would be the *tikkun*, the rabbi laid out four steps:

> "There are four stages to this, and there are no shortcuts. First, you must acknowledge that what you did was wrong. No excuses. It was wrong, full stop." He paused, inviting me to object.
>
> I had nothing to say.
>
> "Second, you must feel—consciously and directly—regret for your actions. I do not say, feel guilty! Not guilt, regret! They are not the same thing. Guilt serves as its own excuse: 'See how bad I am; what

would you expect of someone like me?' Therefore I am free to repeat the offense, since this is just the way I am. It excuses the action by seeing ourselves as the worst we can be.

"Guilt also allows repetition because it serves as self-punishment: 'I feel guilty for what I did. I chastise myself. I've punished myself for the offense; therefore I am free to repeat it.'

"Regret, on the other hand, is not the same as guilt. It is expressed by: 'I can't believe I did that. It's not like me. This is not how I am! How could I do such a thing?' It means to see ourselves as the best we can be, and to be disappointed in not living up to that."...

"And this is the third stage. To be able to say: 'I will not do it again. I have changed. I now have foreknowledge. I will not do this again. Even if brought to that situation again, I would not go through with it. I am a Jew. I will not lower myself to this. Let them carry out their threat.' "

I shivered. Rav Ish-Shalom never broke eye contact. "This is your final destination. This is the port to which you are to sail."

I stared out across a sea impossibly immense, under a starless sky....

"The fourth stage is to reach a point where you can bring all of this before God and say aloud and with absolute conviction, 'I accept full responsibility for what I have done. I have learned and changed. I regret my actions and I will not do it again.' This point can only be reached by going through the previous three stages."[62]

In July 2010, under the rabbi's guidance, Yael did her final act of *tikkun*. In Judaism, if one has sinned against someone who subsequently has died, one must go to the grave with ten witnesses and formally ask forgiveness. Ovadya's victims had no graves, only ashes. Nevertheless, Yael went to Birkenau to ask forgiveness from the dead in front of ten witnesses.[63]

It was a rainy day. There were no men around, but near the memorial beside the Krema was a group of twenty Chassidic high school girls, accompanied by their teachers. Yael approached them and asked if they would be willing to aid in the performance of a mitzvah.

I stepped forward into their circle and with shaking hands took out the handwritten note that I had prepared. There was no time to explain; their bus was waiting for them. I told them that what I was going to read pertained to something that had happened at this very spot sixty-seven years ago.

"You are my witnesses," I said.

A gentle rain fell on the page as I began to read. Tears blurred the Hebrew words on the paper.

11 Tamuz, 5770

In the month of Adar II 5703 the Jews of Saloniki were brought to this place, to Birkenau-Auschwitz.

---

62. Yael Shahar, *Returning*, Apple edition (Alfei Menashe, Israel: Kasva Press, 2018), pp. 384–386.

63. Since she was asking for forgiveness, these witnesses could be female.

I—Ovadya ben Malka—survived for a year and seven months in this place. I survived because I was useful to our enemies. I helped them to murder my people and to conceal their crimes. For more than a year and a half, I worked here in Krema 2 and burned the bodies of those murdered in the gas chambers. Together with them, I burned my world, my humanity, and my name. I was not Ovad-Ya [servant of God] but Eved-HaGermanim [servant of the Germans].

I refused to relinquish my life for Kiddush HaShem [sanctification of God's name], and instead committed Hillul Hashem [profanation of God's name] and a great crime against my people, and especially against my brothers and my sisters whose ashes are scattered all around us here.

Therefore I have come to this place to perform the Viddui [confession] at their grave as required by our Laws, and to tell what happened at this place to the Jews of Europe, murdered here with cruelty that no words can express. I have come to tell what I have not been able to speak aloud until now.

I cannot say with certainty, as the Rambam wrote: "I will never repeat my deeds." I don't know whether I would have the courage now to do what I should have done then. What I do know is the price I have paid, the nightmares and the memories with which I live.

"We have departed from Your Mitzvot and Your laws, and have gained nothing."

—Ovadya ben Malka

The words came out in a different accent than the one these girls were used to, unfamiliar even to me. The voice speaking had grown old and halting, and was choked with tears. I finished and looked up into the tearful eyes of my listeners. It was all I could do to remain on my feet.[64]

Returning from Poland to Israel, Yael wrote: "I had done what I had come to do. I had become the person I was meant to be. My true name is Ovadya, which means 'Servant of God.'"[65] This is true *tikkun*.

---

64. Ibid., pp. 695–697.
65. Ibid., p. 703.

CHAPTER 10

MEETING AGAIN

ACCORDING TO KABBALAH, souls are connected in soul groups and often come back into this world together, in different permutations of relationships. A father can come back as the son or daughter of the souls who were previously his children; a wife can come back as the sibling, child, or husband of her previous spouse. This might explain why sometimes, upon first meeting, two people can feel a sense of recognition or familiarity.

Since the purpose of life is *tikkun*, this reshuffling of relationships is meant to have the rectifying potential of empathizing with the other's situation because one was previously in that role. Or sometimes there is a past debt that needs to be paid or unfinished business that needs to be resolved. At other times, souls from the same soul group encounter each other again ever so briefly, each on its own mission, just for the déjà-vu spark of recognition, like sharing a secret handshake before each goes on his own way.

In addition to such "soul-group reunions," a person may encounter someone who played a pivotal, often negative, role in that person's former life. All such recognitions come from the faculty of intuition, which only in the twenty-first century is beginning to gain scientific credibility. Dr. Judith Orloff is a board-certified psychiatrist and assistant clinical professor of psychiatry at UCLA. In her book *Second Sight*, Dr. Orloff came out of what she calls "the intuitive closet," where she was afraid of "being condemned by a hyper-cerebral world that has forgotten how to see."

Dr. Orloff makes a strong case for the reliability of intuitive knowing, the "synchronicities, déjà vus, and premonitions," that are too often written off as imagination. She corroborates her validation of intuition by describing experiments and studies of intuitive knowing conducted at UCLA, as well as citing the latest scientific findings suggesting that intuition comes from a different part of the brain. As she writes:

> Cutting-edge science associates intuition with a separate "brain" in the gut called the enteric nervous system, a neuronal network that learns and stores information. In addition, Harvard researchers have linked the overall capacity for intuition with the basal ganglia, a part of the brain that informs us something isn't right and we'd better act on it.[66]

---

66. Judith Orloff, MD, *Second Sight: An Intuitive Psychiatrist Tells Her Extraordinary Story and Shows You How to Tap Your Own Inner Wisdom*, reissue edition (New York: Three Rivers Press, 2010), pp. x–xi.

All of the past-life "recognitions" in this chapter come from the faculty of intuition. In *Second Sight,* Dr. Orloff makes the case that while some people have an innate, strong intuitive faculty, enabling them to recognize people and places unknown in this lifetime, all human beings can develop such intuition.

Josh would fit into the first category. A sense of déjà vu has possessed him several times in his life, each time contributing a fragment of what may be pieced together as a coherent past-life account. Born to a Jewish family in Camden, New Jersey, in 1980, Josh majored in Romance languages in college. At the age of twenty, he was studying abroad in Paris. He took the Metro out to the Belleville section of the city. Belleville was at that period a hodgepodge of recent Chinese immigrants, North Africans (both Jewish and Muslim), and very old Jews, mostly from Southeastern Europe.

As he recalls: "As soon as I got to the main street in the area, Rue Belleville, it was like being hit in the forehead with a two-by-four. I had been there before. And it was a horrible, horrible story. I knew immediately it involved Nazis. I spent a lot of time in that area throughout the year I was in Paris, and the feeling never really went away."

A few years later, Josh was living in Lima, Peru. He decided for the first time to take an excursion into the Peruvian Amazon. He boarded a rusty ferryboat for a three-day trip to Iquitos, the largest city in the world not reachable by road. As the ferryboat pulled into port, Josh had an intuition that something was wrong. This, he was sure, was not the port of Iquitos. Feeling uneasy but having no choice, he disembarked

with the rest of the passengers. He took a motorcycle rick-
shaw the two miles to downtown Iquitos.

In the historic center of the city, he spied a different port.
One of the locals explained that this was "the old port," in use
until the 1960s.

> Then I realized that I literally had a map of the
> entire city in my head. This certainly caused me
> a great degree of consternation, being as I was
> strictly a dialectical materialist, with no way to
> understand how I knew what I knew. Nevertheless,
> it was amusing to be able to lead the group I was
> with around the city, proud of my status as a
> seasoned traveler in this place I had never before
> been in this lifetime. I "knew" intuitively somehow
> that I had been there in a previous incarnation
> as a native-Spanish–speaking Moroccan Jew. This
> struck me as bizarre, but it was no more bizarre
> than being thoroughly familiar with the historic
> center of a city I had never been to, four thousand
> miles from my birthplace.
>
> I was quite surprised when I later discovered
> that there had once been a large Jewish communi-
> ty in Iquitos and throughout the Peruvian Amazon.
> The Jews of the Amazon were almost entirely de-
> scended from Moroccan rubber traders who had
> arrived during the Rubber Boom between 1880
> and 1914 from Tangiers and Tetouán in Spanish
> Morocco. Now there is a fair amount of informa-
> tion available on the Internet about them and a

book by Ariel Segal called *Jews of the Amazon*, but
I was totally unaware of the phenomenon when I
first "returned" to Iquitos.

The Moroccan Jews who had emigrated to the Amazon during the Rubber Boom either succeeded or failed, but most of them left after World War I, with many of them moving to France. Thus, Josh's déjà vu in the Belleville section of Paris, where he also felt like he was a Moroccan Jew, could have been from the same incarnation.

Josh has twice encountered people whom he intuited he had known in his Holocaust lifetime. After moving to Tarapoto, in Peru's Amazon region, Josh made friends with a Jewish man from America. Josh, a veteran in Peru, with experience in legal matters and fluency in Spanish, helped this man get set up in Peru, establish residency, start a company, acquire real estate, and so on. It was a mutually beneficial relationship, providing work for Josh, who was broke at the time.

"We both clearly needed each other," declares Josh. "One day we sat on a park bench smoking cigarettes, and I realized we had shared a similar experience in the concentration camps (perhaps minus the cigarettes), where we had helped each other survive through small kindnesses. I absolutely know that I owed him something." A debt paid, an account closed.

His most intense "repeat meeting" occurred with a German client. They first encountered each other at a shop selling coconut water in Tarapoto, close to where the German man lived. He was keen to get to know Josh. Josh, who always feels apprehensive around Germans, was wary of forming a relationship, but he did not reject the German's overtures to meet for business.

Josh ran a legal translation business, and the German man came to him for help. Josh does not speak German, so he started to speak to him in Spanish, but the new client's Spanish was inadequate. Then Josh tried English, also with limited success. Then he tried French, a language in which they were both fluent. As they conversed in French, Josh realized that he had conversed with this person before, in Paris, under very different circumstances.

> While speaking French with this German client, I began receiving knowledge of our interaction in a previous incarnation. I was an older Moroccan Jew living in Belleville. He was a German official. He was deeply depressed because he hated what he was doing, but he had a job to do and he was going to do it. We struck up a friendship of sorts and would meet for coffee at a local café sometimes.
>
> As the German occupation of France tightened, he became progressively more depressed. He deeply resented his life circumstances and felt powerless to change them. Months went by with us meeting like that. Eventually he could no longer save me. I was rounded up and deported. He must have known at our last meeting that this was about to take place, but he did not warn me.
>
> When we had that conversation in French in Tarapoto, something clicked for both of us. We did

not discuss it, but I could see in his eyes that he felt something as much as I did.

The case was interesting. I wanted to help him establish residency in Peru, which is neither expensive nor difficult, but he refused to understand that it couldn't be done in a certain way. It felt like a mirror image of what had happened in that previous lifetime, in which I was the stubborn one who refused to take an easy solution to my problem, such as bribing my way to safety. It was a strange role reversal.

Sitting across a table from him again, I saw that we had been just two people with a tenuous friendship in a terrible situation, and each of us had a role to play. Neither of us felt any ill will toward the other, just a profound sadness.

As far as his *tikkun* in this lifetime, Josh suspects that it has something to do with his children and his religion. The Moroccan Jewish men who came to the Peruvian Amazon during the Rubber Boom were religiously traditional. Nevertheless, due to the dearth of Jewish women, few of whom emigrated to the Amazon and none of whom made it past Brazil, the Jewish rubber traders married local Christian women. According to Jewish law, the offspring of those marriages were not Jewish. After the peak of the Rubber Boom, many Jewish men abandoned their children and returned to Morocco or France, while others stayed and watched the current of assimilation sweep away whatever vestiges of Judaism they had tried to maintain.

Josh was raised in a Reform Jewish family. "Our family was culturally Jewish," he says. "We read the *New York Times*, watched Woody Allen movies, and espoused liberal political causes." While in college, he married a Peruvian Christian woman and moved with her back to Lima. Josh considered himself an atheist. His minimal religious observance consisted of making some kind of Pesach Seder and not eating on Yom Kippur. At the same time, he recalls, "The idea of a child of mine celebrating non-Jewish holidays was anathema to me."

Some fifteen years after moving to Peru, Josh, by then the father of two children, experienced a life-saving miracle that he attributed to Divine intervention. This launched a spiritual quest that eventually brought Josh to full Jewish observance. By this time divorced, Josh decided to move to Israel. But he would not abandon his children. Their mother was not keen on raising them, so Josh sought and received full custody. He wonders whether making that choice to take his children with him may be a *tikkun* for abandoning his children in his previous life.

"I don't know for sure that this is my big *tikkun*," Josh remarks. "I'm not sure we're supposed to know."

Often patterns from past lives repeat in this lifetime, frequently with the same souls. Stephanie Kraft, a hypnotherapist and energy healer, was born to a Catholic family in Washington, DC, in 1971. She was thirty-five years old and married when she had a very vivid Holocaust dream. In the dream she was a Jewish woman, married with a son, some-where in Eastern Europe.

> They were coming to get us. I had found a way to escape. I felt an overwhelming obligation to go and save my husband. I went back to the house and told him to hurry up, that I know the way to get out. But he took too long. They got us, all three of us. The men and women were separated. My husband and son were taken away. I knew we would all be killed. The dream ended.

Stephanie intuited that her husband in this life was the same soul as her husband in the Holocaust life. They subsequently divorced, with Stephanie and her ex-husband sharing custody of their son. Five years later, however, her ex-husband came after her and sued for full custody. Stephanie felt that she was again in danger of losing her son due to the same man. She felt that her *tikkun* this time was to not respond with fear. She worked hard on banishing the voice of fear within her, and fostering instead an attitude of trust and faith in God.

When the court announced its decision, Stephanie was surprised. Not only did she not lose custody of her son, but the court awarded her more days per week of custody. As Stephanie commented, "I didn't even ask for it." Once the pattern of fear—and blame—was broken, a different outcome ensued.

Andrea was born to a Jewish family in Pittsburgh in 1949. Throughout her childhood, she felt that her older sister, Susan, hated her. It was worse than mere sibling rivalry. Andrea felt an animosity from Susan that she could not explain. For years she bristled in her role as the victim of Susan's malicious, unfounded accusations.

As an adult, Andrea did a past-life regression. In it she saw herself, this time as the older sister, with a younger sister whom she identified as Susan. They were in a ghetto during the Holocaust. Starvation was rampant, but Andrea, in her past-life identity, had a ration card and had made a small pot of soup. She saw herself dishing out a bowl of soup for Susan. Then something angered Andrea and she flung the soup toward her younger sister.

Even in the PLR, as she saw the precious liquid spilled on the floor, Andrea felt aghast. How could she waste food when people were dying of starvation! Andrea did not remember what had precipitated her action, but she suddenly understood why Susan hated her in this lifetime.

By the time Andrea did the PLR, Susan was married and living far from Pittsburgh. Two months after the PLR, Andrea was making a wedding for her oldest daughter. Susan and her husband flew back to Pittsburgh for the festivities, including a catered dinner for out-of-town relatives and Shabbat meals at Andrea's house. Resolved to do a *tikkun* for her unforgivable act during the Holocaust, Andrea decided to focus on feeding her sister. She personally served Susan at every meal, going out of her way to bring her extra portions of food.

In the aftermath of her PLR, Andrea also started calling Susan every week. Once she understood that rather than being just the victim of her sister's meanness, she herself bore responsibility for initiating the nasty dynamic between them, their relationship changed. Victim mode is disempowering and does not lead to *tikkun*. Sometimes finding the roots of a dysfunctional relationship in a previous lifetime evens the roles—and the playing field. Both parties end up winning.

Peter Mond was born to a Jewish family in Brighton, England, in 1950. As an adult he did a PLR. "In a past-life regression," he writes, "I experienced being in the Warsaw Ghetto as a teenager whose job was to find food for his family. This involved leaving the ghetto. One day I was caught on the streets of Warsaw and shot in the head. In the PLR session, I broke down and cried for a long time when I remembered my family of then, especially my three sisters. I saw that one is my wife today and two are my daughters."

As Peter's experience illustrates, credence in reincarnation can not only reveal the roots of relationships, but can also expose precious connections that were torn asunder in a past life. Souls stuck in anger and bereavement can then go forward in their journey of *tikkun*, accompanied by the souls they thought they had loved and lost.

Such was the experience of Wendy, born to a Protestant family in Boston in 1950. At the age of twenty, she was a student at Northeastern University in Boston. While attending a big regional meditation gathering, she met Vickie.

> We instantly started holding hands. Something inside me screamed, *Mother, I found you at last.* It was

a deeply desperate feeling—that of a young child, maybe six years old. We literally didn't stop holding each other's hands for more than forty-eight hours. It was really strange. We both had this strong feeling that we had been ripped apart from one another in the Holocaust.

For some time we became close friends. Then life took many turns, as it always does, and gradually Vickie and I lost track of each other. However, to this day I remain so relieved to have found her for a little while.

Robin Moscow was born to a Jewish family in Philadelphia in 1958. From childhood until the age of thirty-three, Robin had a recurring nightmare where she saw her parents being shot to death by machine-gun fire. In a PLR with Carol Bowman, Robin saw that she had died as a six-year-old girl in the Holocaust. She also cognized that her mother in her Holocaust lifetime is her daughter today. Eerily, the day that daughter was born, Robin's recurring nightmare stopped. "Carol suggested," adds Robin, "that she came to help me in this life because she couldn't help me in my last life."

Pamela Singer was born in 1955 in Bourne, Massachusetts. Baptized as a baby, she was raised Southern Baptist. Pamela converted to Judaism in 1988. Four years later, she had a single dream:

I was a music teacher at a Jewish school in Austria, where the students were boarding because of the Nazis. One Friday night, snow was surrounding the cellar-level windows where we had Shabbat dinner, so we decided it was safe enough to light Shabbat candles. Unfortunately, they apparently reflected in the snow, and suddenly we were invaded by the Gestapo. I abandoned my students and ran upstairs to my bedroom, hiding under the bed. Although this was a "dream," I still feel guilty but was in survival mode.

A German soldier found me but gestured for me to stay quiet. After the school was emptied, I ran to a nearby restaurant and was asked if I was the new cook (who apparently hadn't shown up). I said yes, and started cooking on an old black stove. The dream ended.

After my real-life divorce [ten years after the dream], I met a soldier who'd been in the American special forces and was hired as executive director of our synagogue as a security measure, among other things. He is very proud of his German descent and made it clear he was not interested in Judaism in any way; he just did his job. I felt sure he was the soldier who didn't betray me in the dream.

Only once in my research did I come across the phenomenon of "soul mates." Hypnotherapist Fally Klein told of a non-Jewish friend of hers from Kentucky, who, together with her husband, wanted to convert to Judaism. They had studied

Judaism over several years and were already keeping most of the commandments, including the stringencies of Pesach. However, every time they set a date for their dual conversion, the wife backed out at the last minute. This devastated her husband, who was eager to convert.

The wife came to Fally for a PLR because she wanted to discover what was holding her back. Although the woman knew nothing about the Holocaust except what she had learned during one week of Holocaust education in her Kentucky high school, when regressed she went back to a lifetime as a Jew in the Holocaust. Calling herself "Naomi," she saw her husband Zalman, the same soul as her husband in this lifetime. In the first scene, she saw their wedding.

Later, she saw a brick arch. "Everyone's dead. I'm dead," she murmured. "There's poison in the air. I think it's poison."

Fally asked her, "Where are you?"

"Birken!" she replied. She was screaming and reliving the Nazis' taking her children and her husband.

Fally helped her through that life into a state of calmness in the spiritual realm, where she met the soul of her husband, and they were together again. Fally then asked her, "What's this whole attraction to your being Jewish?"

She started screaming at Fally: "I *am* Jewish. I've been Jewish in many lifetimes."

Fally then asked her, "Why did you choose to come down as a non-Jew?"

Again, the woman screamed at Fally: "Do you know what they did to me? They took everything from me! I will not put myself in a position for that to happen again."

Fally persisted: "But I know you've been with your husband before. Why did he agree to come down as a non-Jew? Ask him."

The wife communicated the reply given by her husband's soul: "He says because we are soul mates, and we have work to do together. We don't need to be Jewish to do that work. It's more important for him to be with me to do that work than to be Jewish in this lifetime."

After this PLR, both the wife and husband have a calmer approach to their conversion. They are still living a kind of Jewish life, but they don't feel pressured or rushed to undertake the actual conversion.[67]

A postscript to this account reveals how little a good PLR therapist injects her/himself into the process. As Fally wrote to me:

> When I asked the client where she was, she said, "Birken." I immediately assumed she meant Bergen, as in Bergen-Belsen. But since I never insert myself into the session or lead clients, I kept quiet.
>
> Later on, she described a brick building with train tracks leading into it that had a clock face at the top of an arch.
>
> The night after the session, she sent me a picture of the famous brick building in Auschwitz where the trains arrived. She had never seen these images before, but after the session googled "brick buildings Holocaust," and when this image came up, she recognized it as the one from her PLR.

67. Interview with Fally Klein, December 3, 2017.

I was slightly disappointed because she had said "Birken" in her session, and being that I was convinced she meant Bergen-Belsen, it didn't seem to match up with the image of Auschwitz. But as a PLR facilitator, I've long learned to wait and trust the process.

Within hours, she reached out again to tell me that she was reading up on Auschwitz and read that Birkenau was the section of the camp where the women's gas chambers were located. Which matched *exactly* to her report in the session of feeling poison in the air in a place called "Birken."[68]

Carol Bowman herself had a strange encounter as an adult that made sense only when she did a past-life regression a year later. Carol was born to a Jewish family in Hudson Valley, New York, in 1950. In 1985, Carol was living with her husband and two children in Asheville, North Carolina. Always interested in classical music, she and her husband attended a concert performed by the Amadeus Quartet. All four of the musicians were Jewish men who were in their seventies at the time.

At a reception after the concert, the violinist approached Carol and said that she looked familiar to him. He asked her what her ethnic background was, and she replied that she was Jewish. He looked her in the eye and said portentously,

68. Fally Klein, email to the author, August 20, 2020.

"Everyone should have left Vienna after Kristallnacht. The handwriting was on the wall. We all went to London."

Carol was disconcerted by the strange encounter. A year later she did a PLR. She saw herself as a musical prodigy who as a young girl had left her family in Poland to study at the Conservatory in Vienna. In the PLR, she saw herself and her two children, bereft of everything, about to board a train for the camps. She eventually died in the gas chambers.

In the wake of the PLR, Carol realized that the violinist from the Amadeus Quartet must have been her fellow student in the Conservatory in Vienna in the 1930s. Fifty years later, he was apparently still harboring feelings of frustration and exasperation with her that she had not heeded the warnings and left Vienna with the rest of her musician colleagues.

In terms of her *tikkun*, Carol disclosed:

> I had to learn that I would be safe in this life. Love comes back. One of the most profound lessons for me is that even though I felt I lost everything so unfairly in that life, all has been returned—including the love. I lost my husband and two children in that life, but I feel that through my present family that love has returned. Also, I was born into a loving family in this life, and felt protected—something that I needed to experience after all the trauma from my last life.
>
> It was a huge leap for me to decide to have children. I was afraid to take on the responsibility. When my daughter was an infant, I wouldn't let her out of my sight. My husband and my brother were

encouraging me to go to a movie with my brother and let my husband watch the baby. I held onto the doorjambs, crying, "I don't want to go." I wouldn't leave her.

I had a lot of anger at God. I felt abandoned by God. Reduced to nothing, as the Nazis did with us, I felt betrayed and abandoned. In ninth grade, I asked a Catholic friend, "How can you believe in God?"

She replied, "Because I have faith." That launched my journey to get back to faith. I absolutely believe in a Higher Power. It's been a long journey back.[69]

---

69. Interview with Carol Bowman, March 18, 2018.

CHAPTER 11

FROM DEATH
TO BIRTH

I DID NOT SPEND FIFTEEN YEARS as a monastic member of a Hindu ashram because I was afraid of having children. Or did I?

I was raised in a middle-class Jewish milieu whose ultimate values were education and intellectual achievement. I went to college with the goal of getting a PhD in psychology. I was a mind inside a body, scoffing at the jocks and cheerleaders who saw their essential identities as bodies to be built up, groomed, and pleasured. I had higher aspirations.

But when I went to India for my junior year of college, I found a guru who raised the ceiling of my reality. Sri Gopinath Kaviraj was an eighty-two-year-old Sanskrit scholar and mystic. In a coup as revolutionary as any political takeover, he enthroned a new monarch to rule both my mind and my body: my soul. This hitherto unknown stranger, my soul, was a projection of the infinite cosmic reality, the Absolute. Kaviraj-ji taught me that there are different levels of reality: physical, mental, and spiritual, and that the spiritual level is the highest because it is causal. He taught me how to meditate, which was like handing me the 3D glasses that enabled me to see the movie as the Producer meant it to be seen.

Once I absorbed the truth that my essential identity is a soul that has a mind inside a body, my academic life back in America became a flat film indeed. Ambitious to a fault, I enshrined a new goal for my life: spiritual attainment leading to enlightenment.

I returned from my year in India, got my BA, and the day after graduation joined an ashram in Cohasset, Massachusetts. Nestled on twenty-one acres of woodland, a mile and a half from the ocean, this paradise was America's oldest ashram.

The year was 1970, and the West was frothy with fascination for Eastern spirituality. Gurus (many of them Jews from New York) were sprouting up everywhere. The guru of our ashram, however, was an authentic Indian woman, Srimata Gayatri Devi, who had been teaching Vedanta in America since 1927. We called her Mataji. She called herself "the ego beater." She was a master at exposing and decimating our egotism, pettiness, and conceit. She would say that you have to boil a pot so that the impurities come to the surface, and then skim them off. The paths toward enlightenment we practiced were meditation, *bhakti yoga* (devotion to God), and *karma yoga* (work in the kitchen, the organic vegetable garden, the cottages for retreatants, and the publishing department, which published books by our founder, Swami Paramananda, who died in 1940).

My Aunt Dot, who upbraided me for renouncing the world to become a monastic member of the ashram, would chide me, "What are you escaping from?" I would reply that the ashram, with its loving-but-firm discipline and the spiritual assistance it offered to a colorful cast of "householders" who frequented the ashram, was an escape from nothing.

Still, I would often hear in my head the Janis Joplin lyric, "Freedom's just another word for nothin' left to lose." If a psychiatrist had asked me to free-associate the word *children*, I would have said, "Vulnerable little beings who can die."

The ashram followed the teachings of the nineteenth-century Bengali saint Sri Ramakrishna. An intoxicated lover of God, Sri Ramakrishna had laid out a path that centered on devotion. Every member of the ashram had to choose an *ishta*, a representation of God to whom one could direct one's personal devotion and love. One member chose the Hindu god of love. A Catholic member chose Mary. I chose the Hindu goddess of death.

The Holocaust was the Kingdom of Death, and the Jewish God did not reign there. In truth, I had only the vaguest concept of God from my ten years of afternoon/evening Hebrew school education. God was like my great-grandfather, who had lived somewhere in the Ukraine. I knew his name and believed that he existed, but I had no relationship with him. Moreover, my obsession with the Holocaust made me angry with the Jewish God. I inherently understood that God had to be both omnipotent and caring. A God who did not stop the Holocaust did not fit that job description. If death was the ultimate defeat, then the murder of one and a half million Jewish children was the ultimate indictment against God, who could offer no defense.

The Hindu goddess of death thus attracted me. Hindus call her "Mother Kali." She is depicted as black, wearing a garland of human heads, and has four arms. For Hindus, she embodies the conviction that death is not the ultimate defeat, but simply one more stage in a never-ending process. Hindus believe in the Wheel of Birth and Death. Death always leads to another life, where you pay the karmic debt you incurred last time around. The only way to escape the Wheel of Birth and Death is through *moksha*, spiritual enlightenment.

When I came to the ashram, reincarnation was not part of my worldview. I had no way to explain my dream in fluent German at the age of fourteen, nor my flashback in Vienna, nor my visceral hatred of Germans, nor my obsession with the Holocaust. At the ashram, however, reincarnation was a given, like the law of gravity, and it solved all the riddles that had perplexed me. Obviously, I had died in the Holocaust. And if I was back in this world, so were many of the other victims. What had seemed like six million horrific story endings were instead six million horrific chapter endings.

In fact, in this lifetime my soul had descended into the most peaceful, prosperous, and stable society, the threshold of 1950s America, to parents who were virtuous and loving, and who lived for their children. If my birth was the door to this salubrious life, then the door to that door was my death in the Holocaust. Death was black because you couldn't see past it, but it was not fearsome and horrifying. Death was merely a transition, like taking off your clothes and putting on a different outfit. Worshipping the Hindu goddess of death eventually led me back to the Jewish God.

By 1984, I had been in the ashram fourteen and a half years. I served as personal secretary to the guru, taught Vedanta and meditation during the guru's lengthy absences at our other ashrams, handled the ashram's investments (Chester Carlson, the inventor of xerography, was one of Mataji's disciples and had left the ashram a wealth of Xerox stock), and, in the role of "senior sister," administered the ashram.

We were universalists, believing that all religions led to the same goal. Therefore, we regularly invited representatives of different religions to speak at the ashram's Sunday services in our Temple of the Universal Spirit.

In November of 1984, for the first time, we invited an Orthodox rabbi, Rabbi Joseph Polak. He spoke on "Love of God, Even unto Madness," quoting the great medieval philosopher Maimonides. Although I had gone to Hebrew school two nights a week until I went away to college and I had attended every Shabbat service, I had never heard the words "love of God" in our Conservative synagogue. Moreover, I knew that Maimonides was a mainstream Jewish thinker, not a fringe figure. The Judaism I knew was about tradition, anti-Semitism, Israel, and social activism. It had nothing to do with God.

In shock, I sat there in the Temple of the Universal Spirit listening to Rabbi Polak. *How can this be Judaism,* my mind reeled, *and I never heard of it?*

A few months earlier *A Bridge of Dreams* had been published. This was the 585-page biography I had written about our founder, Swami Paramananda. Our guru loved the book, and as a prize offered me two thousand dollars and two months to go anywhere in the world I wanted. (When I had entered the ashram in 1970, we monastics were given ten dollars per month "pin money," as all our expenses were taken care of. Fifteen years later, we were getting twenty dollars per month.)

Although I had dreams of spending my two-month leave of absence in an exotic getaway like Bora-Bora, Rabbi Polak's lecture eventually led me to Brooklyn's Chassidic enclave of Boro Park. I decided that I wanted to learn about Jewish mysticism. Rabbi Polak referred me to an Orthodox rabbi named Meir Fund. In addition to teaching classes about the soul based on *Derech Hashem,* a classic text by the eighteenth-century Kabbalist Rabbi Moshe Chaim Luzzatto, Rabbi Fund had a small Orthodox congregation that met in a basement synagogue. He invited me to attend the Shabbat morning service.

In some ways the service was like the Conservative services I had frequented in my youth, but they used a different prayer book. I was nostalgically enjoying the service until they came to Psalm 91. They intoned the words in Hebrew as I followed the English translation on the left side of the page:

> I will say of God, "He is my refuge and my fortress; my God, I will trust in Him." For He will deliver you from the ensnaring trap, from devastating pestilence. With His pinion He will cover you, and beneath His wings you will be protected.... Let a thousand encamp at

your side and a myriad at your right hand, but to you they shall not approach. You will merely peer with your eyes and you will see the retribution of the wicked. Because...you have made the Most High your dwelling place. No evil will befall you nor will any plague come near your tent. He will charge His angels for you, to protect you in all your ways....

With every line, an old anger boiled up in me. *Lies! Lies!* I silently raged. *You did not protect me! I did not see the retribution of the wicked! Evil did befall me! Your angels did not protect me! It's all lies!*

At that point, I jumped up and bolted from the synagogue. My feet carried me up and down the streets of Brooklyn, as my mind spewed a diatribe of anger and betrayal. I *had* made God my refuge as a Jew living in Europe. I *had* trusted in God. And He had not protected me, nor my children. The evil *had* overtaken us. How dare they proclaim otherwise!

I realized that in fifteen years at the ashram, I had made my peace with death, but not with suffering.

Eventually I found my way back to the synagogue and waited outside until the services were over. When Rabbi Fund emerged, I told him what had happened. We walked and spoke for a long time. Rabbi Fund's own parents were Holocaust survivors. He offered no facile answers. Rather, he suggested that instead of being the fiery prosecutor cross-examining God, I try to be the impartial juror patiently listening to all the testimonies. He pointed out that Torah Judaism had over three thousand years of wisdom writings, a great deal of testimony, a great deal to learn.

A short time later, Rabbi Fund sent me to Jerusalem, saying that if someone sincerely wanted to learn Torah Judaism, Jerusalem was the place to study. He enrolled me in Neve Yerushalayim, billed as a "yeshivah for English-speaking women with little or no Jewish background."

In Jerusalem, I felt like an arctic tern, which hatches in the northernmost arctic circle, migrates more than eighteen thousand miles to Antarctica on the earth's southern tip, then wings its way back the whole length of the planet to nest in the place from which it originated. Living an Orthodox Jewish life in Jerusalem, my soul had come home.

I was supposed to return to the ashram on August 23. I asked my guru Mataji for an extension so that I could spend the High Holidays in September in Jerusalem. She reluctantly agreed. But I was torn by conflict. Where did my future lie?

Meditating one midnight at the Kotel, I asked God to direct me. The Prophet Elijah, 2,600 years before, had asked for Divine guidance, and received it as "a still, small voice." Meditating at the Kotel, I heard that still, small voice, and it told me to stay in Jerusalem and live the life of a Torah-observant Jew.

But I could not leave the ashram without Mataji's blessing, a blessing never bestowed on monastics who decided to forsake the highest path of renunciation in order to rejoin the world. I had been running the ashram and in charge of its investments. How could I abandon my post? I knew I could not dissolve Mataji's disapproval or my own guilt without a face-to-face meeting, where I could explain to her what was happening within my soul.

It was just three days before Yom Kippur, the Day of Atonement, the holiest day in the Jewish calendar. I determined to fly to meet Mataji to resolve this conflict, and return to Israel in time to celebrate Yom Kippur with a clear mind and settled heart.

The only problem was that Mataji was in Germany. She, with her entourage, was staying for a couple of weeks with a German devotee in her chalet in the Black Forest. How could I go to Germany, that blood-soaked country? How could I not go?

The Black Forest is in the southwestern corner of Germany, near the Swiss border. I decided to fly to Zurich, which was just an hour's ride to where Mataji was staying. I would hardly be in Germany at all.

My money, however, was running out. I did not have the several hundred dollars for a ticket to Zurich. A householder devotee of the ashram back in Massachusetts offered to pay for half of my ticket if Mataji would pay for the other half. I knew Mataji would agree. She wanted to see me. According to my friend Sister Baroda, Mataji wanted to tell me off and straighten me out. I was sure she would be willing to pay. I just had to call her for her approval before booking my ticket for an afternoon flight that day.

I called the number for the Black Forest chalet. It was busy. I called again. Again busy. For two hours I redialed and redialed. The flight to Zurich was scheduled for three o'clock that afternoon. I would have to leave Jerusalem for the Tel Aviv airport at noon. Noon passed as I became increasingly frantic. Busy. Busy. Busy. Clearly the phone was off the hook. In those days before cell phones, there was no other way to reach Mataji or the other people staying in the cottage.

Finally, in desperation, I called the fire department in that village. The fireman who answered the phone was friendly, but did not speak English. It took a precious quarter hour for him to find someone to translate my request. When he understood, the fireman agreed to go over to the chalet.

Twenty minutes later, Sister Sudha called me. Yes, the phone had been carelessly put back in its cradle and was off the hook. Yes, she would ask Mataji if she agreed to pay half my airline ticket. A few minutes later, she returned to the phone. Yes, Mataji would pay. It was 1:15. I had missed the flight to Zurich.

Sister Sudha suggested that I fly to Frankfurt instead. Mataji had devotees in Frankfurt, a couple who routinely visited our ashram. Sudha was sure that they would be willing to pick me up at the Frankfurt airport that evening, let me sleep overnight in their apartment, then drive me to the Black Forest.

Frankfurt. Smack in the middle of Germany. I would have to spend the night in Frankfurt, then drive for hours through Germany, Germany, accursed Germany.

I believed, as I had been taught, that God is the only operative force in the universe. Human beings have free will in the moral sphere, but God's will controls everything else. There are no "accidents." Why had God let the phone be off the hook? Why was God forcing me to do what I had vowed never to do— go to Germany? Why did God want me to land in the middle of Germany, sleep in Germany, travel the length of Germany?

I did it. I faced the monster I had determined to avoid. It did not gobble me up. In fifteen years of inner work, I had grown too big to fit into the monster's mouth. I sat for endless hours in the car, peeved but not overpowered.

We arrived at the cottage at noon Monday. Mataji was sequestered in her quarters. She always spent Monday and Friday mornings in silence, fasting and meditating. Sister Baroda warned me that Mataji had told her the night before that she was going to scold me for capitulating to *maya*, the force of illusion that seduced monastics off their holy path. I waited in trepidation.

At one o'clock, Mataji appeared in the garden. She took me aside and told me that her "inner guidance," which she always contacted in meditation, had just told her that I was doing what was right for me. She blessed me.

Later it struck me: Had I arrived through Zurich the night before, I would have faced a very different attitude.

The next morning, I flew back to Israel. I arrived on the last flight before the airport closed for Yom Kippur. This arctic tern would make no further migrations.

Judaism, unlike Hinduism, Buddhism, and Christianity, considers marriage the highest path to God. According to its tenets, ever since the Holy Temple was destroyed in 70 C.E., union with one's spouse in holiness is the closest one can get to union with God. I got that. And I wanted to get married. I wanted a relationship. I wanted to find my *bashert* (soul mate). The only problem was that marriage was a package deal that included having children. The first commandment God gave to humanity was "Be fruitful and multiply." This means, according to the Jewish sages, having at least one son and one daughter.

I remembered when I had made my decision not to have children. Nine years after coming to the ashram, I went to India with Mataji to visit her ashrams there. I was riding in a ramshackle bus in Darjeeling, traveling with Jairam, the ashram's caretaker. Sitting there as the bus bumped through the streets of Darjeeling, in the foothills of the Himalayas, Jairam asked me, "So, you're satisfied never to have children?"

Having children meant leaving the ashram, being exiled from my spiritual paradise. On the other hand, I felt my biological clock winding down, as I had just turned thirty-one. In those days, few women had their first child much past that age, so it felt like soon or never. Yet the "never" in Jairam's question echoed in my heart.

My belief in reincarnation stripped childhood of its innocence. Each time a soul comes back into this world, it bears the baggage of previous lifetimes. Jack the Ripper as a toddler was neither innocent nor adorable, of this I was sure. How did I know if that rambunctious five-year-old darting around with a runny nose wouldn't grow up to be a murderer or terrorist, or had been a Nazi the last time around? What was so endearing about a small body with a nasty occupant? Having children is dangerous, I told myself. You never knew which soul would come to you, or what would happen if it did.

So, staring out the window at the distant Himalayas, I had answered Jairam with quiet conviction: "Yes, having children is not for me."

Now it was six years later. I was thirty-seven years old and had invested my entire adult life in pursuing a specific goal—enlightenment. The ashram had taught me that children and spiritual practices were incompatible. Even in Jerusalem, I rose early to spend one hour doing yoga and meditating, and another two hours praying the Jewish morning prayers, contemplating the deep import of every word. This regime would be impossible with a crying baby or a meddlesome toddler. I was not willing to throw seventeen years of arduous spiritual practice into the diaper pail.

I took my dilemma to Rabbi Yitzchak Ginsburgh, a highly respected Kabbalist whose weekly class in English I zealously attended. I traveled to Rabbi Ginsburgh's home in rural Israel and sat across a narrow table from him in his family's sparsely furnished living room. His luminous face, framed by his long gray beard, radiated understanding. I was sure he would comprehend my spiritual yearnings.

"I know that Torah-observant Jews have to have children," I complained. "But I'm afraid that if I have children, I will forfeit all my spirituality."

Rabbi Ginsburgh looked at me as if I had made a preposterous equation, as if I had said, "I am afraid that if I get a job, I'll lose all my money."

"Bringing souls down into this world is the highest thing a human being can do," he began. "Souls come from the highest of the ten *Sefirot*—the channels of Divine energy that are manifest in the world. They come from the 'Crown'—*Keter*. There is no way for human beings in this world to access *Keter*, not through the intellect, not even through meditation. But when two souls unite in holiness, they have the potential to actually contact the level of *Keter* and bring down a soul." He then launched into a Kabbalistic explanation that left me far behind.

Although my mind conceded the point, I still resisted. I decided to take my predicament to my ultimate spiritual advisor, the Chassidic Rebbe of Amshinov.

The Amshinover Rebbe embodied the spiritual greatness I was striving to attain. He meditated deeply on every word of every prayer, taking a full two hours to pray *Birkat HaMazon* (Grace after Meals), which most Jews zip through in five minutes. So long did it take him to complete the extensive Shabbat prayers, with all his Kabbalistic meditations on every word, that he usually ended Shabbat on Tuesday.

I had seen the holy Rebbe three times before, always in the middle of the night. The procedure was to request and be granted an appointment on a particular night, then on that night, around midnight, to go to the Rebbe's tiny third-floor apartment in the Jerusalem neighborhood of Bayit Vegan, and to patiently wait my turn. Between three and four in the morning, the frosted glass doors to the dining room, where the Rebbe received his visitors, would slide open, and his gabbai (attendant) would gesture to me to enter.

When I requested an appointment this time, however, I was informed that the procedure had changed. Now the Rebbe was seeing people only during the day. I was told to be there promptly at 2:45 in the afternoon.

The apartment looked totally different with the Rebbe's family (seven daughters at that time) awake and about. Two daughters with long, dark braids passed me on their way to the minuscule kitchen. When the gabbai ushered me into the dining room, I noticed a baby in a pink stretchy standing up in a playpen in the far corner of the room.

The Rebbe rushed in (he always walks fast) and sat down directly across the dining room table from me. I was ready with my question: "Wouldn't taking care of babies be an obstacle to my spiritual attainment?" But before I could speak, the baby in the corner started to wail.

"Excuse me," the Rebbe said, jumping up. He rushed over to the playpen, lifted up the baby, quieted her, carried her back to the table, and sat down again facing me, the baby in his lap.

"Now, what was your question?" the Rebbe asked me kindly, both he and the baby peering earnestly at me.

My question froze in my mouth. God Himself had answered me with the Rebbe's hands-on demonstration.

So, despite my lingering doubts and my subconscious resistance to motherhood, I decided to take a leap of faith into the abyss of marriage and children, hoping that it would be okay. I started dating.

In the Orthodox world, matches are generally made through a rabbi, matchmaker, or friend who arranges for a woman and a man to meet, based on their on-paper compatibility of background, personality, and life goals. The pair goes out, reports back to the matchmaker, and each decides whether to meet again. The matchmaker sets up the first few dates, then the couple is permitted direct telephone contact. Since they are meeting only to answer the question, "Is this the person I want to marry?" the process is focused and brief. After the first, second, or third date, a clear "no" on the part of either the man or the woman ends the match. If they continue to go out five, six, or seven times, engagement is likely to follow.

After a year and a half in Jerusalem, I was still single. I had been set up with several men, none of whom I wanted to see even a second time. In each case, I had a different reason for rejecting the match. Then one night, I had a life-changing dream. I dreamed that I lived in a house with a few other occupants. Someone came to the door to fetch me, to take me on a journey across the sea.

I wanted to embark on this journey, but one of my housemates said that I couldn't go until I had performed my chore. My chore was to go down into the basement and bury the corpses of a mother and her ten dead children. I did it. In the musky darkness of the basement, shovel in hand, I buried the mother and her dead children. Then I came upstairs and announced that I was ready to go on the journey.

When I woke up, I sat straight up in bed and said, out loud to the empty room, "Now I can get married and have children."

Soon after, I was set up with a thirty-nine-year-old musician from California, Leib Yaacov Rigler. We got engaged in eleven days, and two months later we married. Fourteen months after that, at the age of forty, I gave birth to my first child, a daughter. We named her Pliyah, meaning "wonder of God."

My overwhelming feelings during my first months of motherhood were delight and surprise. Holding my baby in my arms, I felt such sheer joy every day that I would break out into laughter. Not a polite snicker, but an open-mouth, head-back laughter. This was always followed by the question: "Why didn't anyone tell me it would be this wonderful?"

My parents had come to Israel for the birth, and Leib's parents arrived a few days afterwards. For our Pesach Seder three weeks after Pliyah's birth, we had not only both sets of parents, but also my beloved friend Paula. Paula had been my college roommate. We had stayed close, through her years at Harvard Medical School, through her move to Palo Alto, where she became a respected oncologist, through her marriage to Michael, and through the birth of her three sons Howard, Ira, and Avi. Having Paula, with Ira and Avi, at our Pesach Seder that year filled me with a sense of completeness. I had left my past incarnation behind me. Or so I thought.

Our small family was sailing along as if in a convertible on a bright spring day when suddenly we hit a brick wall. Six months after Pliyah's birth, I became pregnant with an ectopic pregnancy, a life-threatening condition. My doctor failed to diagnose it, and no one suspected I was pregnant. One night several weeks later, the embryo burst the tube, causing internal hemorrhaging. I didn't know what was happening. Why the terrible pain? Two days later Leib took me back to my ob/gyn. I was barely able to walk. He pronounced that there was nothing wrong with me.

Witnessing my tremendous pain and increasing weakness, my friend Ruthie asked her Kabbalist-mentor if he could "see" what was happening inside me. He said I was pregnant. With that, my doctor ordered a pregnancy test. The results, which came an excruciating thirty-six hours later, confirmed the terrible truth: I was pregnant with an advanced ectopic pregnancy, which could be dealt with only by emergency surgery. Leib rushed me to the emergency room.

The Amshinover Rebbe's mother told me to request a certain top doctor for the surgery, but it was ten o'clock at night and he had just gone off duty. He said that he could perform the surgery only the next morning. The surgeon on duty warned that I could not wait. They operated at eleven o'clock, a four-hour surgery, trying to mop up five days of internal bleeding. When the doctor emerged from the operating room, he told my husband that if they had waited till morning, I would have been dead.

The next five years of my life were a drama with one theme song: trying to have a second child. With just one fallopian tube left and extensive scarring from the ectopic pregnancy, I had to go through endless medical treatments, tests, ultrasounds, and procedures. Each one ended with disappointment.

Concurrently, I tried alternative treatments. Reena, a Yemenite folk healer with a successful track record of helping many dozens of hopeless cases, had in her anteroom five photo albums boasting pictures of smiling babies, all the products of her skill. Her treatment consisted of lighting fires in small jars and then putting them upside down on my abdomen. The fire would suffocate from lack of air, creating a vacuum that pulled the feminine organs up to the surface, where Reena would massage them with her fingers (and long fingernails). Lying on Reena's table, the only thought that enabled me to endure the pain was that I would not have to suffer the pains of Gehinnom (Hell) because I was suffering them now. Reena's treatments left me with welts, but no baby.

Another folk healer was from Afghanistan, with a tradition seven generations in her family. Her massages were more gentle, but no more successful.

While pursuing every medical and alternative lead, I also did everything spiritually possible to have another baby. I prayed at the tombs of countless tzaddikim (holy people). I begged for blessings from living tzaddikim. I gave more than we could afford to charity.

My rebbe, the Rebbe of Amshinov, guided us on our quest. He told me, after yet another failed procedure, "Perhaps the soul that is meant for you is not ready to come down yet." I took this as a veiled promise that there was a soul meant for me who would come down to me at the right time.

I learned in the Bible about the Shunamite woman, a childless woman in ancient Israel who built an upper room on her house to accommodate the prophet Elisha and was then blessed by him to have a child. In our days, I discovered, childless couples would pray for a baby at the site of this "upper room." In our tireless quest for another child, Leib and I drove to the Jezreel Valley in north-central Israel, to the village of Shunam, currently an Arab village.

Unsurprisingly, there were no signs directing us to the site of the house where the prophet Elisha had worked this miracle. Spotting an Arab pedestrian, we stopped our car and, knowing no Arabic, asked in Hebrew, "*Ishah Shunamite*, the Shunamite woman?"

He understood immediately. Apparently, the Arab residents were used to these desperate Jewish couples coming to their village seeking miracles. He directed us to the spot. But when we got there, there was nothing but piles of stone scattered in mud. An Arab nearby explained to us that the house with the upper room had survived all these millennia, but the heavy rains of the previous winter had caused the building to collapse. We stood there, beside the stones and the mud, and beseeched God to have mercy on us and grant us a child.

I also joined a support group for infertile women. Every week we had a guest speaker. One week a psychologist came and delivered an uncomfortable message. She averred that often the obstruction to getting pregnant was not physical but rather psychological. She suggested that we try to discern the psychological block that may be preventing us from getting pregnant.

I went home, my mind sputtering. I knew, but didn't want to face, my mental block. This was the elephant—or rather the Nazi—in the room. I was afraid of losing my children, as I had lost them in the Holocaust. Children were fragile, vulnerable, impossible to protect. Somehow my fear had taken a furlough when I got married and shortly afterwards gave birth to Pliyah. But after the ectopic pregnancy, it reawakened like a hibernating ogre, hungry to devour any child I would bear.

I knew no way to vanquish this ogre, so I gingerly stepped around it while I continued my fertility efforts. When my father died, and then, a year and a half later, my mother, we inherited a small sum. We decided to use it on the ultimate fertility treatment: IVF.

At this point I was forty-five years old. The chances of my getting pregnant with IVF was 5 percent, and the chances of my carrying the pregnancy and giving birth to a live baby was half that. Nevertheless, my Rebbe encouraged us to not give up.

The local IVF clinic at Bikur Cholim Hospital offered two tries for one hefty price. We did IVF one time, and failed. I was worn out from all the fertility drugs, the nightly shots, the daily blood tests and ultrasounds. My friend Penny, a nurse, gave me two injections every night. One time she told me that she couldn't find a place to inject me that didn't have a bruise or a welt. Forty-five and a half, feeling withered and worn, I resolved that the second IVF try would be my last attempt to have another child.

The process of IVF involves taking injections of fertility drugs to create as many ovarian follicles as possible that will become eggs. Then, in a surgical procedure, the doctor extracts all the eggs. She fertilizes them in a petri dish. Those that take, she then, three days later, inserts into the womb.

I bought the fertility drugs, and Penny gave me the injections. Then I went for an ultrasound to see how many eggs I had produced. The minimum for doing IVF is three eggs.

When my turn for the ultrasound came, I was surprised to see that the regular radiologist, a brusque and businesslike man, was not there. Instead, another radiologist, whom I had never seen before, smiled and greeted me. He spent a long time— longer than usual—moving the instrument over my abdomen. Finally, he gently broke the news to me: There were only two eggs, not enough to continue with the IVF. My doctor would not do the surgical extraction for less than three eggs.

So this is how it ends? Five years of medical procedures, financial expenditures, and ardent prayers. Five years of storming heaven. It ends here in the darkened room of the ultrasound clinic for lack of one egg? I looked at this doctor, this stranger, and begged him to fudge the results on his report, to say there were three eggs.

He agreed. Handing me the false report, he blessed me to have a baby.

The next day, when my doctor did the extraction, she found only one egg.

It was a joke. No one does IVF with only one egg. But I was already on the operating table and already had had my epidural. My doctor extracted the one egg, sent it for fertilization, and told me to come back in three days, if the egg actually fertilized.

I am a believer. I believed that God could give me a baby with only one egg. Leib and I went home clutching the shreds of our dream, hoping that even from those shreds a new life could somehow emerge. We had no idea of the hurricane-force winds awaiting us at home.

I walked into our kitchen and noticed that there was a message on our answering machine. I pressed the button to hear the message, and the ogre of my fears jumped out. The voice was my friend Paula's, crying hysterically, "Sara! Call me! Call me!"

With a trembling hand, I dialed Paula's Palo Alto number and heard the dread news. Twelve-year-old Ira was dead. He had gone to a wilderness camp in Utah. Holding a frying pan, sitting on tree roots, he had been struck by lightning.

Ira was dead! Dead! Paula was drowning in a whirlpool of grief. I had to go to her. Forget that one egg in a petri dish, my last chance at having another child! Did I really want another child after all? Children die. This was the motto of my Holocaust-carved fear, now starkly in my face. Children die. There is no way to protect them. No way to save them.

Children equal death, and loss, and grief that doesn't die even when I do.

I called my Rebbe, who had guided us in our fertility efforts throughout these five years. Paula needed me. I wanted to freeze the one egg and fly to her.

The Rebbe asked me to inquire of my doctor whether freezing the egg meant it would have less of a chance of succeeding. I asked her, all the while snickering because it had almost no chance of succeeding anyway. My doctor responded that of course freezing lessened the prospect of success. The Rebbe told me not to fly to Palo Alto at this time, that I could go later, but now I should follow through with the IVF.

The egg fertilized. I went back to the hospital. As my very secular doctor inserted the one egg into my womb, she instructed me, "Pray."

The next two weeks were a wrestling match between my desires and my fears. I wanted a child. But children die. I wanted a child. But Ira had died. I wanted a child. But did I have the courage and the strength to face a fate I could not control?

One day, sitting in my bedroom, the ogre of my fear stood before me. I did not flee. Instead, I faced the ogre and said to myself, *If I have a child and he dies, can I continue to believe in God and the goodness of God?*

Throughout this lifetime, God had been so good to me. Could my faith in God's goodness survive the death (again) of my child? Could I see the canvas of my life as awash with good even if it were spotted with dots of black? As I contemplated this question, I felt a steel-like strength arise within me. The more it grew, the more the ogre of my fear shrank.

Finally, I made a bargain with God. The Sages of the Talmud debate which blessing one should say upon hearing news of the death of a close relative. Since everything God does is ultimately for the good, the optimum blessing would be, "Blessed is God, who is good and does good." But human beings, when faced with pain and loss, cannot see the truth of God's goodness clearly, so the Sages concluded that bereaved individuals should say, "Blessed is God, the True Judge."

Sitting in my bedroom, watching the ogre of my fear shrink, I made a vow to God: "If You give me a baby, and he lives to the age of twelve years old—twelve years of seeing, hearing, walking, thinking, talking—I will rejoice in the goodness You have granted me. I will relish the blessings of every one of his years, weeks, and days. And after that, if You take him, I will say, 'Blessed is God, who is good and does good.'"

With that, I vanquished the fear, the ogre, and the Nazis who had haunted my life. For me, on that day, the Holocaust ended.

Nine months later I gave birth to a healthy baby boy.